TWELVE AND ONE-HALF KEYS

TWELVE AND ONE-HALF KEYS

To the gates of paradise

written and illuminated

by

edward hays

Forest of Peace Books, Inc.

OTHER BOOKS BY THE AUTHOR:
(available from Forest of Peace Books, Inc.)

Prayers for the Domestic Church
Prayers for the Servants of God
Secular Sanctity
Pray All Ways
Sundancer

TWELVE AND ONE-HALF KEYS

copyright © 1981, by Edward M. Hays

Library of Congress Catalog Card Number: 81-50505
ISBN 0-939516-00-4

published by
Forest of Peace Books, Inc.
Route One — Box 247
Easton, Kansas 66020

printed by
Hall Directory, Inc.
Topeka, Kansas 66608

first printing: February 1981
second printing: June 1983

cover design by
Edward Hays

dedicated

to my Mother and Father who,
by the stories they told me,
both educated and entertained me . . .

and to the little boy and the
little girl in each of us who,
after our parents,
are our greatest teachers.

grateful acknowledgment

to Richard and Patricia Wilson who,
with reassuring affection,
encouraged the printing of these
stories . . .

to Thomas Turkle whose
editorial skills and time
were invaluable in preparing them
for publication . . .

and to David DeRusseau whose
artistic judgment with the art work
was of great assistance.

the parable-stories

A Prayer Rug Introduction

They tell a Sufi story about a poor, but honest, jeweler who was arrested for a crime he never committed. He was placed in a high and well-protected prison in the center of the city. One day, after he had been imprisoned for months, his wife came to the main gate. She told the guards how her husband, the poor jeweler, was a devout and prayerful man. He would be lost without his simple prayer rug. Would they not allow him to have this single possession? The guards agreed that it would be harmless and gave him the prayer rug. Five times daily he would unroll his rug and pray.

Weeks passed, and one day the jeweler said to his jailers: "I am bored sitting here day after day with nothing to do. I am a good jeweler and, if you will let me have some pieces of metal and some simple tools, I will make you jewelry. You could then sell what I make in the bazaar and add to your low salaries as jailers. I ask for little — just something to fill the idle hours and to keep my skill in practice."

The poorly-paid jailers agreed that it would be a good arrangement. Each day they brought to the jeweler some bits of silver and metal and some simple tools. Each night they would remove the tools and metal and take home the jewelry that he had made. Days grew into weeks; weeks into months. One bright morning when they came to the jeweler's cell, they found it empty! No sign was found of the prisoner or of how he had escaped from this well-protected prison.

Some time later, the real criminal was arrested for the crime of which the poor jeweler had been falsely accused. One day in the city's bazaar, long after that, one of the guards saw the ex-prisoner, the jeweler. Quickly explaining that the real criminal had been caught, he asked the jeweler how he had escaped. The jeweler proceeded to tell the amazing story.

His wife had gone to the main architect who had designed the prison. She obtained from him the blueprints of the cell doors and the locks. She then had a design woven into a prayer rug. Each day as he would pray, his head would touch the rug. Slowly, he began to see that there was a design, within a design, within another design, and that it was the design of the lock of his cell door. From the bits of leftover metal and his simple tools, he fashioned a key and escaped!

The stories that follow in this book are keys that will unlock for you the gates of paradise, as the poor jeweler's key gave him freedom. But, like the jeweler's key, these stories will not give immediate entrance. You will have to pray over, ponder upon, and reflect beyond the story you read. I suggest that you only read one story at a time. If the parable-key does not immediately open to the mystery, be patient. Return again and again to turn it — first this way and then that — before throwing it away or simply thinking of it as only interesting.

For parables and fairy tales are puzzles which are often difficult and strange to us. Frequently, parables are puzzles which are intended to mystify. If they are resolved too quickly, then they are no fun to play with. They are puzzles to amuse; and from them we may shape and create the most mystical and spiritual of all signs, the question mark!

A parable is a puzzle that runs parallel to a truth or to several interlocking truths. Usually they run parallel to a great truth which is not easily expressed directly. Stories teach us about the truly important things in life, and it is highly possible that "great truths" are only learned by stories! Since a story or parable deals with eternal truths, it will have several levels. That is what makes rereading so enjoyable. Each time, we have the possibility of reading the story at a new and more mystical level.

The prophet Isaiah presented a puzzle when he said, "Look and you will not see, listen and you will not hear. . . ." Fairy tales and parables deal with what cannot be seen and cannot be heard, but which we can see and hear if we know the key.

The purpose of these stories is not simply to teach. Stories also entertain, delight, and heal us. In ancient India, when persons came for the healing of an emotional sickness, they were given a fairy tale. They were told to take it home and reflect upon its meaning. Within the story was the good medicine that would allow them to escape from the prison of sickness in which they found themselves held prisoner.

In his visionary Revelation, the beloved apostle John beheld a vision of the Eternal City, Jerusalem. The vision of heaven was of a city, beautiful to behold: "Its walls, massive and high, had twelve gates at which twelve angels were stationed. Twelve names were written on the gates. . . ." (Rev. 21:12) May these twelve and one-half stories be keys to unlock those gates of Mystic Beauty.

Illuminated, But Not Illustrated

This book of parables and fairy tales is not illustrated for a good reason. The modern storybook is often illustrated, and so fails to create magic for the child or the child within the adult. Every illustration is but how one person, the artist, sees what is happening. An illustration, more often than not, is a distraction! The artist's idea of what the words express can easily block the reader's imagination from creating an inner image. Parables and fairy tales heal; and part of the healing lies in the image created within the reader and not in the picture printed on the page.

Tolkien, the famous creator of the modern magical tale, felt the same. To him, the illustrator did little to aid the reader. Tolkien believed, and rightly so, that when an author speaks of the deep woods the reader's imagination does not see some individual forest, but rather a forest composed of all the woods, forests, and groves he or she has ever seen — especially the woods which first gave flesh to that word for the reader.

So this small, simple book shall enjoy illuminations to delight the heart, but no illustrations to block the imagination. May you, the reader, find within its pages magic, wonder, and healing.

Books must be read
as
deliberately
and
reservedly
as they
are
written.

Henry Thoreau

Chin Lin

Once upon a time, there was a beautiful woman named Chin Lin. Each day, before sunrise, she peddled her bicycle through the soft, turquoise-blue twilight of pre-dawn to her job at the Red Dragon Chinese Restaurant. There she was employed as a baker and waitress. But her most important work was neither of these; it was the writing of fortunes for the fortune cookies that she baked each day.

Each morning, Chin Lin unlocked the back door of the darkly deserted, silent kitchen of the Chinese restaurant. Taking a straw mat from a closet, she walked to the center of the kitchen and unrolled the mat, facing the single window that opened to the east. She bowed deeply and took her place on the mat. Surrounded by ovens, stoves, work tables, and racks of pots and pans, she prayed. Each day, before her work began or the others arrived, she entered into meditation as the rising sun slowly chinned itself on the rooftops of the city.

Twenty or perhaps thirty minutes later, as the kitchen was filled with the yellow warmth of sunrise, she arose, bowed deeply, and replaced her mat in the closet. Seated at one of the kitchen tables, she took pen in hand and began to write. Usually the fortunes came quickly, in a rush of words. Unknown faces formed on the empty, white paper, and each fortune she wrote was uniquely personal. For Chin Lin there were no anonymous fortunes. It took only a few swift moments and she was finished. Chin Lin was inspired.

By this time, the narrow alley outside the restaurant was bubbling with bustle and noise — garbage trucks, delivery vans, and the arrival of her fellow workers. The day at the Red Dragon Chinese Restaurant had begun. Soon the kitchen, too, was filled with activity. The fat, jolly, Buddha-looking cook switched on his transistor radio as Chin Lin carefully placed the small, white pieces of folded paper, with their individual fortunes, into the cookie dough that she had prepared. The sounds of American folk-rock blended with the banging of pots and pans as won ton soup and sweet-and-sour pork began to be prepared. With a mystic smile, Chin Lin slipped her tray of fortune cookies into the hot oven.

Much later in the day, her baking finished, she changed clothing. She took off her working clothes and put on her waitress uniform. Then she left the busy kitchen exploding with the aromas of roasting duck, pineapple, soy sauce, and fried rice.

Now, Chin Lin was no ordinary waitress, as I am sure you have already guessed. Her vocation in life was to be a messenger. As a waitress, however, she appeared and acted like any other waitress in any other Chinese restaurant. When the dinner guests finished their meal and were sipping their tea, she would come and clear away their dishes; bowing and smiling to their compliments about the marvelous meals that were customary at the Red Dragon.

During the meal, Chin Lin would carefully watch each of

the guests in the dining room — watch them with her third eye, the inner eye of the heart, which she opened each morning in her meditation. Having completed their meal, she would carefully select from her collection of cookies the correct one for each guest. Since she had baked them, she knew which fortune was inside which cookie. Now, her heart filled to the brim with reverence and awe, she would place in front of each guest a small blue-and-white plate decorated with ancient Chinese characters. In the center of each plate was a single, lone fortune cookie.

The following scene rarely changed. With smiles and jokes, the dinner guests would break open their cookies and read their fortunes. With some prompting from one another, they would share what was written on the tiny pieces of paper. Laughter and some discussion followed as the small messages about the future were casually placed beside the empty tea cups. With the broken fortune cookies left on the plate, the guests would rise and leave.

This evening, that pattern changed. Chin Lin had waited on a young couple in their early-twenties as they enjoyed a dinner of sweet-and-sour shrimp. At the end of their meal she carefully selected their fortunes and served them. They both opened them and, reading them to each other, smiled. The young woman then rose and excused herself to visit the rest room. While she was gone, the young man read and re-read his fortune — and then quickly placed the small, white paper in his mouth and ate it! Next, he took a tiny bite from his fortune cookie, and placed the remainder of it in his pocket. As his date returned he rose, and together they left the restaurant. Chin Lin was filled with great joy, because she knew that he had understood the secret!

You see, fortunes come true for those who believe in them. At weight machines, fortune-tellers, and Chinese restaurants people read their fortunes, smile, and say, "Wouldn't that be nice!" Then they put that fortune aside and return to their dull, daily lives. They leave their fortunes and their futures to others; to the fates or Lady Luck. But Chin Lin knew; she knew what others did not. She knew that fortunes are surrounded by the food necessary to make them come true. Each fortune must be fed, and in her ancient Chinese recipe for cookies was found the essence of life. The cookie that surrounds the fortune, or wish, was like the fruit that surrounds the seeds of an apple. The function of the fruit of the apple is to be food for the seeds contained in its heart. Each wish and each fortune, like a seed, is life. Where there are no wishes, there is no life!

Chin Lin smiled as she remembered the fortune that she had written for the young man. The small, white slip of paper he had eaten had written on it: "You will die a happy man." That night at the restaurant, he had wondered, "Perhaps I will die tonight! If so, I must make this the most beautiful, love-filled night of my life!"

He did not die, and the next morning he rose, recalled the mystic message, and took another small bite from the fortune cookie which he had placed with great care in the top drawer of his dresser. Days followed days, weeks collected on top of weeks, and years passed in procession as each morning he wondered, "Perhaps I will die today." Each day he took a bite of the fortune cookie; yet, somehow, there never was an end to it. The cookie was never completely consumed. It was both mystical and magical. Daily, he focused his energies on being happy — for he never knew whether this might be the day of his death.

Sixty years after that dinner date at the Red Dragon Chinese Restaurant, he died peacefully in his sleep. At his wake, everyone — and he had an army of friends — said the same thing: "Without a doubt, he was the happiest man I ever knew!"

The Banjo Man

*T*he rising sun was a yellow silhouette in the early morning mist as David jogged along the lonely country road. He preferred this old, dusty road to run on rather than anything else available in the city. Each day, just at dawn, he would drive his car to the edge of town and park. Then he would begin his daily jogging. This morning, he felt keenly the balanced rhythm of his body as his legs moved in perfect precision. Muscles, bones, and nerves all moved in such beautiful harmony. His feet took turns touching the earth — touching, lifting-off, touching again — in a pounding pattern that cleansed his mind.

As he ran this morning, he saw a narrow, winding road that led off to the right from the main road. "Strange," he thought, "that I haven't noticed that little path before." He felt an inner urge, and with ease he turned off the main road and began to jog down the strange little lane. The narrow road soon led into a deep and dark woods. The giant oaks arched overhead, and the early morning sun shot shafts of yellow light through the dense green foliage. He seemed

27

to be in the very middle of the woods when suddenly he felt a sharp pain in his left foot. Ahead, perhaps thirty feet, he saw a fallen tree beside the road. David decided to stop there to rest his foot.

As he sat on the old fallen tree and rubbed his foot, his mind was filled with a rush of thoughts. This morning his thoughts seemed clearer than ever before. They were not new thoughts, only clearer than before: "What shall I do with my life? What will be my life's work? It was so much simpler in the ancient days. The choices were easier: knight, clergyman, merchant, or peasant. A son did the work of his father. But today so many choices are present; and which choice is the right one?"

As David let these thoughts circle in his mind he heard, so faintly at first and then stronger, the sound of music — banjo music! Turning, he looked down the lane and saw a man dressed in a wrinkled, white suit, wearing dark sunglasses and a black sea captain's cap, strolling up this narrow forest lane. The stranger was playing a banjo, and the plunking music was marvelous. When the stranger with the banjo reached the tree where David was seated, he stopped and greeted him, "Good morning. Something wrong with your foot?"

"Yeah," said David. "I think that I must have turned it or something."

"Ah," replied the stranger, "let me have a look at it." Gently laying aside his banjo, the stranger knelt and began to examine David's foot. Surrounding the stranger was a unique aroma that seemed to be a combination of candle wax and incense.

"Allow me to try an old Chinese cure," he said, as he took a canteen from a pack that hung around his shoulder. He then proceeded to pour clean, cool water on David's foot, and slowly began to massage it. His fingers held magic, it seemed, as they worked the muscles of the bottom of the foot and then began to massage the ankle. Even the toes, one by one, were gently but firmly kneaded. The sensation was magnificent. David's entire body was at peace.

He inquired of the stranger, "Would you mind doing the other foot?"

"Not at all," replied the banjo man. When he had finished, all pain was gone. Not simply the pain in his foot, but all pain vanished; and in its place was almost perfect bliss.

"Stranger," said David, "that may be an old cure, but it has to be the most peaceful and relaxing thing that I have ever experienced."

"Our feet are very important," emphasized the stranger. "All the organs and muscles in our body have nerve endings in our feet. Hundreds of thousands of tiny nerves all gather there from the different parts of the body. Not only that, but our feet are what keep us rooted to the earth. The Chinese knew that even the inner-person was reached by way of the foot.

"There, I believe that you are now ready to continue. My work is finished." The stranger stood up and wiped his hands dry on a towel from his shoulder pack. Smiling, he picked up his banjo and began to play.

As soon as his fingers touched the strings of the banjo, music filled the woods and an electric charge shot upward through David's entire body. Without thought, his feet began to move — and suddenly he was dancing! Not simply his feet, but rather his entire body was dancing: legs, muscles, heart, mind, and even his spirit. The stranger bowed to David and, smiling, began to walk away playing his banjo. David started off in the other direction for home; only now he wasn't jogging, he was dancing.

"How marvelous," thought David. "It's so easy and effortless." David had always wanted to dance. He loved music, but found it difficult to be free on the dance floor. He felt stiff and self-conscious and found dancing to be difficult. Now it was different as he danced down the country road. His partners in this early morning dance were the sun, the trees, and the wild grasses along the road. . .in fact, everything seemed to be moving to the melody of the banjo music that flooded his ears and heart.

As he danced along the road toward the city, he came upon a car that was parked off to the side of the road. The driver was in the midst of changing a tire. Printed on the door of the olive-green car were the words — *Army Recruiter.* David danced up to the man who was tightening the lugs on the wheel and asked, "Do you need any help, friend?"

The man stood up, the left side of his uniform heavy with service ribbons, and answered, "Thanks anyway, son, but I'm finished. Instead, can I help you? Uncle Sam wants you!" As he said this, he pointed his long finger at David.

David was delighted! To think that Uncle Sam wanted *him*; he had never thought about the fact that he wanted him personally! (Now, all this time, David had been dancing around in circles to the music that only he could hear.)

The Army recruiter asked, "Son, you some kind of boxer or something? I mean, what's all this dancing around?"

"No, I just feel like dancing," said David. "Isn't it marvelous? Can Uncle Sam use a good dancer?"

"Son," snapped the recruiter, "feet are made for marching, not for dancing; that is, except on Saturday night. Feet are for marching; marching into battle."

"No, thanks," said David. "I appreciate Uncle Sam's invitation, but I prefer dancing to marching." With that, he bowed, and with a large smile went off dancing down the road.

About a mile or so down the road he came to a monastery. He danced up to the front gate and rang the great bell. As the door opened, he asked the old monk who stood there, "I was wondering if the Church might want me, since Uncle Sam wasn't interested?"

The monk was delighted, since vocations had been slim lately, and here was a healthy-looking young man. The monk rushed off to find the abbot. Within minutes, the abbot and several aged monks came to the door. David stood — or, rather, danced — in small but interlocking circles about the threshold.

The abbot spoke: "This isn't Arthur Murray's dance studio, and so if you wouldn't mind standing still, we might consider you as a candidate to this holy monastery. What's the matter, my son, are you nervous or something?"

"Oh, no, Father Abbot," replied David, "but dancing is so beautiful! I've been praying ever since sunrise just by dancing. I am so much at peace with God, with the world and everything, that I feel I should devote my entire life to the Church."

The abbot looked shocked as he replied, "Dancing, young man, is not part of the spiritual exercises of the Church."

At that moment, from up in the sky, there came a loud voice: "Blessed are the feet of those who announce the Good News. Romans 10:15."

David looked up, as did the monks. The abbot did not. He only frowned and said in a tight, steely voice, "That's only Brother Sebastian; he's a hermit who lives up there in the bell tower of the church. Don't mind him; he spends too much time alone instead of in community." All the monks, like the seven dwarfs, nodded their heads in silent agreement with the abbot. "Feet are made for kneeling or tramping grapes in the wine press, but not for dancing," added the abbot, with a tone of final authority.

"Well, sorry. Thanks, anyway," said David, as he turned and, with a little wave and smile to the old monks, danced off down the road, his ears flooded with banjo music.

As he danced along the road, David thought that his questions that morning had been answered, but not as he expected. It really didn't seem important what you do in life; it's how you do it! If you do it with harmony and in harmony, all is beautiful and all is prayerful. "But even a dancer has to eat," he thought. "Uncle Sam didn't want me, the Church didn't want me. . . perhaps I should offer my services to the business world."

Some distance down the road from the monastery was a large soft drink bottling plant. *COLA KING* was spelled out in giant letters on the rooftop of the large factory. He entered the front office and asked if they had need of a young man who was willing to work hard. The secretary was about to answer no, when a junior vice-president spotted the young man doing a soft-shoe dance in front of the secretary's desk. He called out to her to please have the young man wait. He rushed into the office of the president and said, "J.B., I've found the perfect man for our new ad!" And within moments David was ushered into the large executive office.

From behind a two-dollar cigar, the president said, "Young man, you've got promise! I believe we can make you a star and a rich man. We want you to work for us."

"Good," answered a delighted David, "since Uncle Sam and the Church didn't want me. What can I do for you?"

J.B.'s voice spoke from behind a cloud of cigar smoke, "We'll make you famous, son. You will appear in a brand-new ad we're running on television. In this ad, you're just an ordinary All-American kid; then you take a drink from Cola King and suddenly . . . you begin to dance down the street. People see you and want to follow. They all start drinking Cola King and suddenly they're dancing too; everyone is dancing down the street!"

"Wow!" said David. "That's fantastic. You mean that your Cola King can make people dance, can set them free, and put them in harmony with all the earth?"

"No, of course not!" said the president. "Don't be stupid. I thought you were a smart kid. It's just a gimmick to make people buy what they really don't need. But, son, that's business. Right?"

"I'm sorry. No, thanks," replied David regretfully. "I'm not interested in selling people what they don't need and pretending that it will make them dance or be happy." So out of the world of business danced David. But in place after place, he met the same negative response.

Broke, out of work, and alone, he also lost the sound of the banjo music. His dance step became only a slow, silent shuffle. Depressed and lonely, he found himself passing a church and decided to go inside. Entering the darkness, he found a place to sit on a chair that was against the wall, facing a large crucifix that hung behind the altar. His feet were tired and the music was gone from his body as he sat there looking up at the Christ-figure. Strange, he hadn't noticed before that Christ's feet were nailed to the cross. His attention had always been on the hands or head. He buried his head in his hands in sorrow. His feet pained him now as if they had been nailed.

Suddenly he felt someone untying his running shoes, and looking down he couldn't believe what he saw. Quickly, he looked up again at the cross. . . the figure from the cross was missing! Looking down again, he saw the Christ-figure kneeling in front of him. With His tears He washed David's feet, and then began to slowly massage them. As He kneaded the tired muscles, the pain and frustration ebbed out of his body. The Christ-figure did not speak a word but only hummed softly. David recognized the melody as being the same one that the banjo man had played in the woods that morning. Once again, as the figure from the cross massaged his feet, he felt the flow of energy returning to his body. With gentleness, the Christ-figure took David's hand and led him into the sanctuary. Music began — organs and banjos, trumpets and drums — an unseen orchestra playing while the two figures danced in whirling, rhythmic circles.

"Now I know how Jupiter or the planet Earth feels," David thought ecstatically, as he circled around the radiant Christ-figure. Like atoms and molecules, he and the Christ-figure danced in harmony to a blur of vigil lights that flickered in the darkened church. Now he understood that all energy is dance. "Matter isn't some *thing*," he thought. "It's simply energy dancing, from the largest planets to the smallest subatomic particles. All is dance, and those who dance are in the fullest of communion."

With the suddenness of lightning, the darkness was shattered as the lights of the altar area were turned on. Police officers rushed in from both sides of the altar, together with a black-cassocked, old priest.

"Enough of this sacrilege!" shouted the old priest, as the police handcuffed David. While they secured his hands, David attempted to explain about the Christ-figure inviting him to dance. As he spoke, he looked up only to see that the figure was hanging on the cross, His feet once again nailed to the wood and His head hung in sorrow.

This is a sacred place, and you have violated it by this profane dancing and God knows what else," said the priest, his fist raised in anger. David said nothing. He remembered the words of the old hermit who lived in the bell tower of the monastery: "Blessed are the feet of those who announce the Good News."

"Yes," thought David. "Harmony and dance — that's the Good News. Of course, but it is so simple that I failed to understand. Everything is in harmony . . . everything and everyone dancing. Now I know the truth and I shall never stop dancing again, in good times or in bad."

And so, with a smile, David danced down the main aisle of the church, escorted on either side by two large policemen. The priest turned out the lights and left by the sacristy door. The police placed David in their car and drove off.

The church janitor, who from the darkness of the back of the church had seen all that had taken place from the time when David entered the church until he was taken away, came down the aisle carrying his broom. He knelt prostrate in front of the altar and, rising, winked at the Christ-figure on the cross, who smiled back at him. Then, carefully putting his broom away in the closet, he took out a banjo and slipped out the sidedoor.

The Moon Maiden

ecently, in a small Midwestern town, there unfolded a most unusual story. It concerns an early-morning arrest made by the police, just after midnight. Numerous phone calls had been received at the station desk about the strange behavior of a young woman who was seen dancing on her front lawn. She was either drunk or drugged, the callers implied. Without the assistance of either music or a partner, she was to be seen whirling around her yard under the spotlight of the full moon. The police arrived and found the neighbors, clad in pajamas and robes, out on their porches watching the young woman who was gracefully circling the yard like some giant, white butterfly. Now, dancing is not against the law, the good people thought, but whirling about in the moonlight without any music to be heard is surely abnormal — even if it be on one's own front lawn — and must be in defiance of some legal ordinance.

As the young woman, who did not respond to any of the questions of the police, was placed in the rear seat of the police car, the neighbors edged up to the officers, shaking

39

their heads. "Nothing like living in a college town," one of them said. "That kid is some kind of kook; she must be on drugs. This isn't the only weird thing she's done — why, nightly, she can be seen moon-bathing!"

"Moon-bathing?" asked the policeman, as if he had mis-understood.

"Yes, officer," replied a woman in hair curlers. "Out there, on her back lawn. Every night for the past two weeks she'd be out wearing nothing but a swimsuit, laying in the moonlight for hours at a time. Did'ja notice how white her skin is? The law oughta do something about such crazy people being out loose in public!"

Now, as the young woman was booked at the police station, she spoke freely and appeared to be perfectly normal. She told the desk sergeant that her name was Virginia, that she was unmarried, and was a college student. Virginia was booked on charges of disturbing the peace and suspicion of drug abuse, even though no visual sign of any drugs was present. Lacking the money for bond, she was led away by the jailer to a cell; and as he locked the door he saw her walk over to the barred window and wave at the moon!

The next morning in the courtroom she came before Judge Rigur; who, being up for re-election, had firmly preset his mind on how he was going to handle this drug offender, so as to set an example for that college crowd. Her court-appointed lawyer sat mutely beside her as Judge Rigur asked if she pleaded guilty to the charge of drug abuse; and, if not, how she would explain her dancing on the front lawn and moon-bathing in the back yard. Virginia, dressed in white and beaming radiantly, stood before the judge and began her bizarre story.

"Several weeks ago, Your Honor, I was driving home alone late at night. Suddenly, my car just stopped. It was strange — as if somewhere out in space someone had thrown a switch and all engines had stopped! It was as if all the laws of internal combustion had just been thrown out of the textbooks! Well, I didn't even try to start my car, but got out and started to walk home. As I walked along, I became aware that the moon was following me. It would appear from behind a housetop and wink at me or it would suddenly spring up above some giant oak tree and beam at me. I realized, as I walked along, that the moon wasn't just playing hide-and-seek, Your Honor — the moon was flirting with me! That's when I began to moon-bathe. I found great pleasure in just-being alone with the moon."

She paused briefly in her story to clear her throat. The judge, lawyers, and others in the courtroom all leaned forward lest they miss a single word.

"Several weeks later. . . just last night. . ." Virginia continued, "the very same thing happened to my car; I mean about the laws of internal combustion being turned off. As I began to walk home, the moon again began to flirt. I became entranced at how full, how round and perfect it was; how clean, pure, and white. As I came to the corner of Seventh and Kentucky, where that small park is, I felt compelled to go into the park. There I found the moon luring me towards a clearing in the midst of the tall trees. The small clearing was filled with white light. At that moment, I knew that I was in love with the moon, and more unbelievable — the moon was in love with me! That night, there in the park, the moon made love to me! When I finally arrived home, I was as full as the moon, and I just had to dance. And, Your Honor, the night air was filled with music — with silent music!"

Jumping to his feet, her attorney shouted: "Your Honor! This is not a case of drug abuse or even of disturbance of the peace — this is a case of seduction. This poor, innocent girl has been raped by the moon! I demand that before we go any further, the Full Moon be made to appear in this court-room!" So the judge, glad for some excuse to delay the pro-ceedings, adjourned the court and instructed that a warrant be issued for the arrest of the Full Moon.

Police cars fanned-out that night across the city in search of a Full Moon, but found none. None, at least, that fit the description by Virginia of being "perfectly round, white. . . ." Indeed, they found a moon, but not the one specified in the warrant. Finally, in frustration, they arrested (as is often the case) the only moon they could find.

News of the affair had raced through the town, and the next morning Judge Rigur's courtroom was packed with the curious as the moon took the stand. Alongside her attorney, sat Virginia, dressed again in white and wearing a huge, circu-lar, white straw hat. When asked by the court to state its full name, the moon replied, "Less-than-Full." Asked again by the judge if it was not really the Full Moon, it again replied, "No, I am Less-than-Full."

To all other questions, whether from the judge or from the attorneys, it would now only sing, "Shine on, shine on Harvest Moon. . . ," or other moon songs like, "I'm only a Paper Moon. . . ." Judge Rigur pounded his gavel as the moon sang on and Virginia began to dance, a streak of whirling white, before the bench. The judge's gavel broke off at the handle as he pounded it, demanding order in the court. Both the moon and Virginia were charged with contempt of court and placed in jail.

The court convened again after one of those long holiday weekends. But the moon looked different, as if it were losing weight; it was, uh, smaller, or thinner. Now, when asked its name, the moon replied, "Half-Moon." And upon further in-terrogation it began to sing, "When the moon comes over the mountain . . .," and, sure enough, Virginia began to dance again.

Judge Rigur became furious: "I will not tolerate such foolishness in my court!" He summoned the sheriff and inquired if the moon were fasting, and the sheriff replied that the moon had not eaten a thing since it was jailed. The judge demanded that the moon stop fasting, and also that it stop singing songs.

The city attorney now called a series of witnesses in an attempt to bring some sense, if not order, to the case. The first one was a psychiatrist, who appeared with an armful of charts and diagrams which conclusively proved that it is impossible for anyone, male or female, to biologically and physiologically enter into sexual relations with the moon. Also, he stated, it is impossible to love anything other than another human. Beer, sports, even one's dog, cannot be loved; one can only be fond of such non-human objects. He speculated that somewhere in Virginia's childhood was the root of this moon-obsession.

The next witness was a minister of the Church, who clutched a large black bible in his left hand as he mounted the stand. The Reverend broke into one of those Sunday-morning-stained-glass voices as he spoke of behavior such as Virginia's as being "unnatural"; loving other than what is intended. His voice rose to a pentecostal pitch as he ranted about "the lust, the immorality of today's young people!" He went on to say that he had checked with Virginia's neighbors and found that she did not attend church regularly on Sundays either. "And all this business about the moon making love, and sex in groves of trees, is diabolical. The Bible tells us that only that which is natural is intended, and all else is sin." As he spoke, his eyes flashed with the particular glint of those whose lives oscillate between prayer and pornography. Only with great difficulty did the judge finally end the preacher's mini-sermon to the court.

Next, the prosecuting attorney called Virginia's boy friend to the stand and inquired if he had been with her on the night in question. Her boy friend, who appeared a bit un-nerved at the experience of being cross-examined, testified that he had not seen Virginia on that night. In fact, he told the court, he worked nights as a janitor at the university, and so knew nothing of any of this.

Through all of this, Virginia sat smiling, the picture of equanimity and beauty. The moon also sat smiling; at least, what was left of him did, for he was now referred to as "Quarter-Moon." Noticeable to all in the court was the fact that as the moon grew thinner, Virginia grew fatter — she was pregnant!

The parade of witnesses continued. Several stated that they had not seen a moon that night or were unsure if it was out. They stated that actually they seldom looked out-side at night. Others remarked that they did not see the moon, but that they had seen Johnny Carson.

Virginia's attorney called three witnesses to the stand in her defense. The first was a young couple who had been parked, on the night in question, on a hilltop just outside of town. They saw the full moon and remembered how perfect it was. To them the moon seemed to say that all was good, that they were good, and that their love for one another was as good and as beautiful as the full moon itself.

Next to be called was a prisoner from the jail. Yes, he had also seen the moon that night. As he stood at his cell win-dow, it appeared over the roof of the Sears building, full and round. It had filled his naked, dingy cell with beauty, and it filled his heart with hope as well. Yes, he remembered the moon and how it had spoken to him.

The last witness for the defense was somewhat unusual she was a lady of the night. Yes, she also had seen the moon that night and remembered it well. Her last customer had gone home, and she was standing at her window. To her the moon appeared not only beautiful, but perfect and pure. The white light of the moon had washed her body, and she felt clean, good, and whole. . . both in body and soul.

The courtroom was in turmoil. The testimony had been so contradictory that it seemed the judge, society, religion, and even reason itself were on trial instead of Virginia.

As the judge adjourned the court, the moon appeared positively emaciated; it was just a skinny sliver as it and Virginia were led back to their cells.

About eight o'clock the next night, the jailer rushed to the sheriff with news that the prisoner Moon had escaped. They both ran to the prisoner's cell; it was dark and empty, and there was no moon. Nor was the escaped prisoner to be seen anywhere in the town or the whole county. Though there was no moon of any size or description to now convict of a crime, the judge, frayed and weary, decided that tomorrow he would end the case and pronounce a judgement.

The next morning he called Virginia before the bench and asked her if she had any statement to make before he gave his judgement. Standing there, radiant and beautiful, dressed in white as always, Virginia began to sing:
"I am filled with the greatness of light,
        and the joy of the Harvest Moon
        floods my heart.
For the Moon has looked upon me,
        a simple and common girl,
        with love and great affection.
The Moon that is mighty,
        that pulls the great ocean tides,

and causes earthly things to grow up
from the soil,
has made me fertile and full.
The Moon makes fools of the intellectually proud;
and pious, churchy people are unseated
from their pews.
But the prisoner, the prostitute,
the poet, and the poor —
those hungry for love and beauty —
dance by its light
and are fed as if at a banquet."

Slowly turning around, speaking to all the courtroom, she said:

"And because the Moon who is great has so loved
me, I love you and ask that the Moon shine
on all of you with great grace and peace."

She then bowed her head and was silent.

The judge was joined by the minister, the doctor, and the sheriff as he pronounced her guilty of being a fool and a lunatic. The doctor charged her with being a terrorist who had attempted to kidnap reason and mortally wound science. The minister charged that she was a security risk to the Church, a threat to morality and to the conscience of innocent children. The sheriff declared that she was a malignant cancer, a risk to peace and order.

"What would happen," they all chimed in, "if everyone began to dance and sing whenever and wherever they wished — on lawns, streets, in courtooms?" They all agreed she was guilty and should be hung until dead. And so she was, by the four of them, on the back steps of the courthouse.

Now, after she died, three nights of total darkness followed. There was no moon to be seen; the only lights in the sky were tiny stars. But on the fourth night, there appeared over a small town in midwestern Kansas a new moon — just a sliver, a baby moon. And next to the silver sliver — the crescent new moon — was a beautiful, blue, glistening star. Three astronomers back east at the Yale Observatory, who had been watching the night sky, remarked about the size and brilliance of the star and the freshness of the moon-child, and they wondered at what it might mean.

And Judge Rigur, who was washing his hands at the kitchen sink, looked out his west window, and seeing the new moon . . . wondered what it all meant.

The Stranger's Bargain

*I*t had been the last show of the night as the young man walked out of the theater showing *Star Wars*. "What a neat, neat movie," he thought to himself. It had been a long time since he had been so moved by a motion picture. He climbed into his battered, but good, old blue '66 Chevy and turned the key. The engine sputtered and coughed . . . then backfired and died. He tried it again and again, giving it more and more gas. Finally, it died altogether and refused to make a sound. Climbing out of the car he opened the hood, saying out loud as he did, "She must be flooded!"

"That's what it sounds like to me," came a voice from over his left shoulder. Turning, he saw a handsome man who appeared to be in his mid- to late-thirties, with beautiful blond hair, standing beside a shiny, black van parked next to his car. Looking around, he saw that they were the only two left in the parking lot; the other cars were all headed homeward. The handsome, tanned stranger asked, "Can I be of any assistance?"

The young man could not remember when he had last

seen such a handsome man as was this stranger, and he responded, "No, thanks. I'm sure that it's just flooded; just a matter of time and then I'll try again, but thanks anyway. Were you also at *Star Wars*?"

"No," replied the stranger as he lit up a cigarette. "I don't care for movies; too much unreality for me. I'm not into the fantasy bit!"

"Oh," said the young man, "I see. What are you into?"

The stranger took a long drag on his cigarette and, smiling, said, "You might say I'm a buyer. I'm in the swap-and-shop business!"

"Really?" replied the young man. "What do you buy?"

"Perhaps if I tell you my name, it might be easy for you to guess what I buy. I am . . . the Devil! Oh, don't look so surprised; it's true. Yes, that's who I am; and more important, I have been waiting just for you, young man. I have a special deal that you won't be able to turn down. I believe you will find that to accept my offer will be of great personal benefit to you."

"Suppose I do believe that you are who you say you are? I guess then that what you want to buy is my soul!"

"Hardly, although I must confess that's the common belief. I mean that the Devil is interested in souls. Never could understand how that myth began. But I assure you, it is not true; I do not buy secondhand souls." The stranger moved closer and sat on the front fender of the young man's Chevy as he continued, "Yes, I know all about Faust, Dorian Gray, and all the other stories of people who have sold their souls to the Devil for power, knowledge, or to keep themselves youthful forever. That's fiction, son. No, that's not the business deal I had in mind for you!"

The young man raised one hand in a symbol of "wait-a-minute" and said, "Even if I was willing to make a deal with you . . . if you are not interested in buying my soul, what do you want to buy? Surely not my old '66 Chevy?"

"Correct. You're a sharp young man. I do not buy secondhand souls or secondhand cars; my business is Dreams. What I want to buy from you is your Dream."

"My dream?" said the young man. "Well, let's see, I had a real dilly last night. You see, I dreamt that I played the saxaphone in a Masonic marching band, and . . . ."

"No, no, no." interrupted the Devil. "I'm not in the market for sleep-dreams or even day-dreams. What I buy is *the* Dream; that special vision of how you see yourself as an adult in this world. That Dream first appeared in your late teen years, and in it you are a star, you are a hero. Your life has cosmic dimensions. Your stardom has to do with greatness because your Dream has such great possibilities for the future. That Dream fuels your life with meaning and a rare form of excitement. It is that Dream that sets you apart from the others; in fact, from everyone else!"

"I don't understand," said the young man. "Why would you want to buy my Dream and not my soul?"

"Because, my young friend, if I were to obtain your soul I would have just a soul, but if I am able to purchase — at a fair price, mind you — your Dream, then I have changed the course of history! Your soul affects only you, but your Dream — ah, that's something different. Your Dream touches the lives of countless people and, who knows, maybe people yet to be born? The effect of your Dream is cosmic, and that's why I am interested in it."

"Humph! A cosmic Dream riding around in a '66 klunker! I'm not making fun of you, understand, but I would guess that there must be only certain people, special types, that have these cosmic Dreams that you're so interested in."

"No, on the contrary, my friend," replied the Devil, as

he flicked the remains of his cigarette, like some tiny, white missile, out into the darkness of the parking lot. "Everyone, at one time in their life, has such a Dream. Everyone is a closet hero or heroine. Every woman and man dreams of being someone special, of being great or unique: in sports, movies, politics . . . even the Dream to be a great plumber or a great mother. But between sixteen and twenty-six, or perhaps even thirty-six, they trade in that Great Dream for a little dream, an average dream. Some don't though, and then together we work out a good arrangement that serves both of us well; that is, most of them are open to an arrangement, although a few refuse. There was this guy, a long time ago, named Moses; had this crazy Dream about liberation for a bunch of no-good, and even thankless, brickmakers . . . yet just wouldn't sell it. But you don't win 'em all. Right, kid?"

Before the young man could answer, the Dark Stranger continued, "Those people who settle for an average dream don't have a Dream to sell. Since in early adulthood their Dream was out of harmony, sort of unconnected to their real life, it simply died. When the Dream died, there died with it a sense of being alive and of having any real purpose in life. By the time I arrive with my special offer, both the dreamer and the Dream are dead. The dreamer is not officially dead, understand . . . but the life is out of him. And another problem is that girls are not supposed to have Dreams; I mean no special or Great Dreams, but only ordinary, average dreams. So from the first they do not have much of a chance to keep any Dream afloat."

The young man found the conversation so interesting that he forgot about attempting to start his car. Motioning with his eyes for him to continue, the mysterious stranger went on.

"People like you, my friend, are of real interest to me.

Your Dream is still alive. In fact, right now it is extremely healthy since you just came out of that accursed place over there."

"You mean the movie theater?"

"Correct. I hate movies, for they are Dream-food. They fill dreamers like you with the nonsense of being heroes or heroines. Movies like *Star Wars*, or even the old-fashioned cowboy movies, reawaken the Dream in people to be something other than ordinary. It's a magic world inside there; a world where Dreams are possible. I had hoped that TV would kill the movies as well as the Dream-life. Those commercials every few minutes prevent you from Dreaming; they chop up the magic and make it simply entertainment.

"But people keep going to the movies, and so I keep traveling the road in my van, offering my special deals. But business is bad recently; a shortage of Dreams. Take a few years back when the cultural dream was the way to be a hero: get married, settle down, raise a family, and work at some dumb job for a lifetime for the sake of the kids. Not anymore; no one considers that to be special or heroic.

"Then we had the period of the anti-cultural hero. It was the anti-social dream of greatness: the 'opt-out, do-your-own-thing" bit. March in the streets against the government, the war, or some other social cause. Today, no one thinks about a protestor as being a hero or heroine. With the Ku Klux Klan, middle-class taxpayers, and freako-Nazis marching in the streets, all protestors begin to look silly, not heroic!

"Today, lad, is the age of the un-hero — who is somewhat like the un-cola. It's not by accident that Woody Allen, the arch-un-hero, won an Oscar for his movie. Take my word for it, it's a sign of the times!

"Yep, it's sad. Look around this parking lot; no one to do business with but you, son. You're among the few."

There was silence for awhile, and then the young man asked a question, "What happens to people with dead Dreams?"

"They usually marry other people who have dead Dreams; it works out better that way. And if one of the partners has a Dream that is just barely alive, and the other partner has a dead Dream, the dead Dream will smother what's left of the life in the good Dream.

"What's interesting, from a professional point of view, is what happens when people with different and opposite Dreams marry. Ah, a head-on collision and the result is divorce. The usual mistake in marriage is that attention is focused on sexual compatibility instead of Dream compatibility. Lovers would be better off if they spent more time dreaming together instead of making-out so much. But excuse me, I got carried away. You see, I usually don't discuss the more technical aspects of my trade with potential customers. But you're a good listener, and I can see you're interested."

"You're right, and for a Devil I find you to be an interesting person, but I have another question. I could understand if you, as a Devil, were interested in buying a Dream if it was religious. But I don't understand why you would want any Dream; you know, like Dreams to be a great engineer, doctor, or artist? I thought Gods and Devils were into the spiritual realms?"

"Son, every cosmic Dream is religious regardless of how that Dream is lived out. All Dreams are about God or, if not, then about some god. People are just as religious today as they were in the Middle Ages, only they worship different gods: money, success, power, looks, sex. But, of course, any smart kid like you knows that these gods are impotent. They pale in the face of infinity or even in the face of plain, old death. Death makes the gods of modern religion look silly." The handsome stranger lit up another cigarette and smiled, saying, "While we're waiting for your carburetor to settle down, care for a ride in my van?"

"Thanks, anyway," said the young man, who at this point had no desire to even see inside that mysterious, windowless black van. "But I do have another question. It's back to the original question I asked — what happens to people with dead Dreams?"

"To be perfectly honest with you," said the Dark Stranger, " — and there are those who believe that I rarely am — people whose Dreams have died, soon die themselves. For most of them, if their Dream dies, at say age twenty-five, it may take another forty years for them to be buried; but they're just as dead as if they had been buried at age twenty-five! Did you know, son, that every day on this planet there are one thousand suicides? And that at least ten thousand other people attempt to hurry up their deaths? Your Dream is the lifeline to your soul; kill your Dream and it is only a matter of time until you will want to die yourself!"

"That's terrible!" responded the young man. "Don't you feel any guilt or shame for such a waste of life?"

"Don't blame me, like I was some sort of fiend. By the time I arrive, hoping for a little business deal, there's no Dream left. It's parents, society, school, church, the realists, or people who don't like change — they've done most of the dirty work. Don't blame me. I would like to find some good Dreams around. I have some terrific values and good deals, that much you have to say. When I take a Dream, at least I always give 'em something of value in return."

"No offense," said the young man, "but I have a hunch that the dream you give in exchange, after a few years, turns into a nightmare!"

"Perhaps, but you have to admit that for those few years it's really great being on top! How about it? You're an intelligent young man. I know what it is that you really desire and I promise you: give me your Dream, and what you have desired will be yours . . . now, tonight!"

The young man felt uneasy. Even in the darkness of that deserted parking lot he could feel the intense glance of the eyes of that stranger staring right into the center of his soul. He was overwhelmed with the temptation to say "yes," but he closed his eyes to avoid the piercing stare. Why not; why not sell his extraordinary Dream?

For some strange reason, he suddenly remembered a line from a movie he had seen a couple of weeks ago, *Equus*. Like *Star Wars*, it had been a great movie. Richard Burton, as a psychiatrist, had those great lines as he reflected upon curing a young man: "The normal is the good smile in a child's eyes, all right. It is also the dead stare in a million adults. It is the ordinary made beautiful; it is also the average made lethal."

Standing by his old '66 blue Chevy, in that empty parking lot with the neon words of the theater marquee now black and silent, he knew. He knew that the Dream his heart held had been placed there by God. The Dream had to do with being God-like; that's what it means to be a hero or to be a heroine. That was the Dream that this man, or whatever he was, wanted. And that was the very Dream that society also wanted to kill.

It was precisely this Dream — this ability to be God-like, to be holy — that he, and perhaps everyone, felt so ambivalent about — so ying and yangy, hot and cold. Our spiritual possibilities fascinate us, but at the same time we are fearful of those possibilities. We are attracted toward them and at the same time repelled, even defensive, if asked about

58

them. Who knows, perhaps this is part of the anguish of being human . . . this ambivalence about realizing the God-dream that lives within us?

"No, stranger; no, thanks. I don't think my Dream is for sale or trade."

There was no smile on the stranger's face as he said, "Better think it over, son. Because even if I do not have the power to take away your Dream by force, I can make you wish that you had done business with me.

"Remember that carpenter from Nazareth? He wouldn't sell his Dream and you remember how he ended up? Or take the case of that young French girl, Joan of Arc? She made the same mistake and her Dream went up in a puff of smoke . . . and she with it! Or Martin Luther King — his Dream was shattered with a high-powered rifle bullet. Better think it over, kid, tonight. . . ."

The heart of the young man was pounding wildly as he felt the overwhelming power of Evil coiling around him like some giant snake. He felt his ability to refuse frozen. He closed his eyes and did something he hadn't done since he was a child — slowly, over himself, he made the sign of the cross.

As he did, for some reason he remembered a quotation. The words of it were clear and filled with confidence: "Do not be intimidated; do not be afraid of anything. You are worth more than an entire flock of sparrows!"

Suddenly he heard the engine of the van start up, then the loud peeling of rubber and the roar of the engine as the black van raced off into the dark, moonless night. And just as suddenly, and without any effort on his part, the old '66 Chevy's engine began to idle with a warm purr.

As he drove home that night he thought seriously about his Dream. What was it, really? How was he special and what was his unique gift to the world? He also thought about the offer the Devil had made, and also about his threat. Turning into his driveway, he gave a great sigh of relief that he had escaped with his Dream and soul unharmed. But then he remembered the closing words in St. Luke's gospel about the time that the Devil came to tempt Jesus when he was in the desert . . . and maybe, just maybe? As he climbed into bed the words swirled around him: ". . . having exhausted all these ways of tempting him, the Devil left him . . . to await another opportunity."

The King's Wizard

*I*f you look very closely at the figures on a chessboard, you will find to your surprise that they are all smiling. This perpetual smile is something that was not always the case.

Once upon a time — long, long ago — there was a great disturbance in the realm of the White King. The King stomped his foot and filled the palace with angry shouts: "Where is 'today'? I demand to know! Has someone stolen 'today'? I am not sure how long it has been missing; you see, I have been so busy of late that I have paid little attention to it. The last time I remember seeing 'today' is about two weeks ago. Where could it have gone? What, oh what, will my life be like if I never see it again?"

The Queen turned to the King and, attempting to lift his gloom, said, "Tomorrow, my Liege, we shall go shopping . . . tomorrow. Or we can take a trip . . . next week. I've been planning this redecoration of . . . ." The Queen talked on and on, but her words were all of tomorrow. Secretly, the Queen thought that "today" was dull and all too common.

The Queen's Knight spoke up and said, "Her Ladyship is

right, my Lord. Tomorrow is where your attention ought to rest. Forget this obsession with the possession of today; the entire world can be yours! Let your mind feast upon these plans for a royal war: With banners flying and the sound of trumpets filling the air, we shall march across that short stretch of territory and defeat your ancient enemy, the Black King. Then the future will proclaim you the 'Great King.' "

"Your Royal Majesty," spoke up the Bishop, who was dressed in yesterday's clothes, "in the beginning . . . and the ancient ones said unto us . . . remember when, as it was written long ago . . . ." The Bishop spoke not of today but only of yesterday and the holy events of long, long ago. Puffs of dust, like gray clouds of incense, rose up from his paragraphs. The pawns hung on his every word and, when he had finished speaking, made the sign of the cross upon themselves with pious devotion.

The pawns said nothing about the absence of today and did nothing about it. The pawns couldn't move forward or backward unless someone moved them. They were noble but silent servants who knew little about the existence of today. As slaves, they blotted out today and thought only of yesterday when they were not pawns but free people. Or they dreamed of tomorrow when they would be free again and could do whatever they wished. For a slave, today is so filled with pain that one must — if one wishes to survive — think either of yesterday or tomorrow. They would always listen with eager ears to the Bishop, for he was able to speak about yesterday and to fill their hearts with dreams about the great tomorrow and the rewards it would hold for accepting the sufferings of slavery; for resigning themselves to the pains of today. The pawns said nothing; they only stood there waiting patiently to be told what to do next.

As the Queen, Knight, and Bishop were all speaking at the same time, the King, boiling over, shouted, "Quiet! What I want is today, and all I hear is talk of tomorrow or yesterday. I want today — the present moment!"

At that very instant, with a flash of golden light and a puff of purple smoke, there appeared in the exact center of the board a Wizard who, in seeming madness, made his way down the center line between the two kingdoms. He turned and walked right through the center of the mass of white pawns, passed their ordered ranks, and headed straight for the King. The pawns did not make a move, but waited, as was their custom, for orders. Both the Knight and the Bishop began to move forward to stop this intruder, but the piercing eyes of the Wizard froze them in their squares.

Not so the Queen (her heart had felt frostbite for so long that she was unaffected by the mystic look of the Wizard). His glance only glided off her white, glacier face, and she demanded in authoritarian tones, "Who in the world are you? Whoever heard of a Wizard in a checkered kingdom? What possible business could you have here?"

The Wizard bowed with grace and humor, saying, "Your Ladyship, my work is to stand next to the King — invisible to the casual observer — and to counsel him by whispering into his ear the Truth. Call me his guru, his poet-confessor, his jester-confidant; if not, Your Highness, his intimate comrade."

Delighted with this sudden turn of events, the King invited, "Come quickly, Wizard, here beside me, for I need thee. I am surrounded by knaves and pious fools. Oh, Wizard, you are the answer to a prayer. You see, I have lost today. No, I have misplaced it. No, rather, I am the victim of a violent crime, for someone has stolen my today. Help me, please!"

The Wizard, leaning upon his tall oak staff, suggested, "Perhaps, my Liege, you are only at the mercy of an energy shortage! In this modern age we are running out of food, oil, and gas; as well as peace, saints, and heroes. Is it not possible that we have all just run out of todays? As a result, all we have left are the by-products of today: yesterday and tomorrow; synthetics made up mostly of dreams and promises. Then again, it is not impossible, Sire, that perhaps your today, the Royal Present Moment, was stolen!"

"I knew it!" exclaimed the King, his crown sliding over his left ear. "I am the victim of a violent crime! Who is responsible?"

The Queen cried out in her operatic voice, "This theft is a crime against the Crown . . . hang the thief!"

The Bishop appeared on the balcony and announced in a solemn voice to the pawns, "This is a Mortal Sin!"

The Knight mounted his steed with the cry, "This is the work of the Black King. We must strike back; we must retaliate! Soldiers, prepare for war!"

The King, at first caught up in all the excitement, exclaimed, "Yes, this must all be so! This must be the act of some extremist group. Revolutionary terrorists have kidnapped my today. I will empty the royal treasury to pay a ransom."

"Indeed," wondered the King, "is the stealing of today a royal crime? What if? . . . yes, what if only kings can own today; if only kings had todays that could be stolen?" Lost in his thoughts, the King mused to himself, "Of course! That's why no one else missed today . . . neither the Bishop, Knight, nor Queen. That's why no one else was alarmed . . . only kings know the delight of today!"

The Wizard (because he was a wizard) knew the thoughts of the King, and at length spoke up: "That is not entirely true, my Liege; though, indeed, most people do not have a today. A king here, an Arabian prince there, but also 'little people' can own todays; as can poets and lovers, saints and heroes, and a hermit here or there. Silent people usually own a today, as do fishermen and mystics. The thieves who steal today are not terrorists, but robbers with names like 'fame,' 'success,' and 'busy-busy.' And then there is the professional archthief: 'Speech.' Since speech, ninety percent of the time, deals only with the past or the future, it secretly steals away today. People who are not compulsive talkers, who know the art of silence, seldom suffer the loss of today."

"Oh, Wizard," whined the King, "what will happen to me if I am unable to recover my today?"

"My Liege, you will become ill," responded the Wizard, "and sickness will possess you. Sickness is caused by dis-ease. Since one can only be 'at ease' in the present moment, it is, in reality, impossible to be so in either the past or the future." At this point the Wizard was speaking directly into the royal ear, and the Bishop and the Knight were leaning at almost ninety-degree angles in an attempt to hear. The Wizard whispered, "We need a celebration, some festival, in order to return us to the present. For we can only celebrate in the present moment. We can only dance in the 'now.' We can only sing songs and flow with the music in the present. We can only make love today . . . we need, my Liege, a feast!"

The King's face shone like a spring sunrise. "I have a royal idea," he proclaimed, as everyone listened with expectant ears. "We shall declare a festival, a Feast of Today. We have Mother's Day and Father's Day and all those other 'Days' whose names I can't remember, so why not a 'Today Day'? I therefore do solemnly declare this to be 'National

Today Day!' Fly all the flags and let stamps be printed to commemorate the glories of Today!"

The Wizard bowed to the King, saying, "A marvelous idea, my Liege; a stroke of royal genius. Healing and long-standing health will surely come if you can be absorbed into the celebration of Today. And besides, the Crown can make a mint off the tourists who will come to share in this ingenious folk festival. We can sell calendars with only the present day on them and clocks with no hands. And since there will be no time to prepare for a future war, peace will fill the land. Truly a smashing idea, my Liege!"

And so the King did declare a "Feast of the Here and Now," a "Holiday of Today," and placed his seal upon the royal decree with such authority that the force shook the entire palace. "No thinking of yesterday!" exclaimed the King, startling the Bishop, who was lighting candles in remembrance of some ancient feast. "No thinking of tomorrow!" he proclaimed again, so shocking the Queen that she dropped her Sears and Roebuck catalogue with which she had been dreaming of what she was going to buy next week.

The King continued, "Let all my subjects celebrate the pleasures of the present. Everyone shall greet one another with 'Happy Today!' " This greeting filled the land, and "Merry Moment!" or "A Pleasant Present to you and all your kin!" came the replies.

Then a surprising thing happened — the white pawns all ran to the neutral zone at the center of the board. Throwing down their swords, they began to dance and have a picnic with the black pawns. (This is not really all that surprising since they were cousins anyway, and it was only because they were told to go to war that they ever fought each other in the first place.) The Black Bishop and the

White Bishop met at the center line and received Holy Communion together. The Black Queen and White Queen shared afternoon tea. Both Kings moved among the crowds, attended by their Knights. One King would ask, "What time is it?" and the Queen's Knight would answer, "Now, my Lord!" Then the other King would ask, "And where are we?" and the King's Knight would chime in, "Here, my Lord, here!"

And so laughter and song, mixed with merriment, filled the entire land, and the King was happy because his today had returned and everyone — Kings, Queens, Bishops, Knights, and pawns — could enjoy the present moment. And because the pulse of the present throbbed in everyone's veins, there was no sickness anywhere in the kingdom. (And that is why, even to the present, you will not find a doctor on a chessboard.)

On and on went the Feast of Today. Everyone dined and danced for hours, then everyone stopped for a period of silence. Sitting very still, they all chanted their private mantras: "now, now, now, now . . . ." And they tried to think only of the "now," the present moment. After fifteen minutes or so, the bells rang and all returned to the Celebration of Today. Every six hours the bells would ring again . . . and once more all would become silent.

But the King was fearful that today might be stolen again or even misplaced. "How," he thought, "am I to prevent another such tragedy?" This time the Bishop had an idea.

"Let us make a new sacrament," he proposed, "a Holy Sacrament to remember today by celebrating the glories of today only. We shall call this sacrament 'Vacation,' and, by Law of the Church, it shall be received not once a year but at least once a week, or as often as possible!" The bells in the cathedral towers rang out, and the King led the loud applause of all the people. Such a wind was stirred up by the applause and the swinging of the bells that all the candles in the cathedral were blown out!

And so everyone in the chessboard realm lived happily ever after. The life in the kingdom became one of stop and go, feasting and fasting . . . and never as it had been with only go, go, go.

At the conclusion of one of the periods of silence, the King, in a resplendent smile, addressed the people: "My kingdom is only in the present moment. Only those who are willing to live in that precious moment, in the now, can be my servants. Those who lose today shall lose me. Fear not the future; regret not, nor dwell upon, the past . . . for in me there is neither past nor future. Rather, they have become fused as one in the present moment."

All the players on the chessboard were perfectly still, each content and happy within his or her own square and forever living only in the present moment . . . forever moving, striving, acting, celebrating, and being still — today.

The Secret Agent

*T*he day was typically heavenly; the weather, as always, was divine, as well it should be in heaven. God, however, seated upon the Great Golden Throne, was deep in thought. More than simple thinking, God was filled with curiosity. God knew what was going on everywhere in all of creation; everywhere, that is, except in one place. God was curious about what was going on in hell! God did not know and could not know. For, you see, if ever a part of God — even the Divine Knowledge — was in hell, it would cease to be hell, since hell is the total absence of God!

This was no recent problem for the Lord God; for centuries, it seemed, God had wondered. Finally, on this day, He decided something must be done. But what? That was the question. So, like any good administrator, God called a meeting.

From every part of heaven they came — angels and archangels, saints and bearded prophets, apostles, and even Jesus and His mother, Mary. When all was quiet, God shared the great divine problem with them: "What in hell is going on?

Since it was created eons ago and I closed the iron gates, I have had no knowledge of that place. Who knows, perhaps it has been redecorated or even air-conditioned? I have other questions as well. After all these centuries, my curiosity is too much. I have decided just now — since that is the only time that exists here anyway — to send someone down there as a spy, as my Divine Secret Agent. This secret agent can see what is going on and return to give me and all of us a complete report."

The prophet Jeremiah spoke up: "Lord Yahweh, I will go. You've sent me before, send me now!"

The patriarch Moses, his great white beard glistening in the light from the Golden Throne, spoke with great authority and in a voice filled with the majesty of Mount Sinai: "My Lord Yahweh, as You sent me down into Egypt to set free Your Chosen Children, send me now to be Your agent in hell."

"I've been through fire, shipwreck, and prison for You," shouted Saint Paul, "and I'm ready for hell. That's one crowd I would love to preach to!"

A multitude of voices rose from the crowd around the Golden Throne, all volunteering.

God scanned the saintly crowd with its hundreds of raised hands and said, "Thank you, all of you. Thank you, Mohammed, for your kind offer . . . and you, Buddha, thank you as well. But for this most special — if not impossible — mission I will, I think, ask Mary, the mother of Jesus, to go to hell for me."

"My Lord God," said the Blessed Mother, "You never cease to amaze me with impossible missions. First, You asked me to be the mother of Your Son, Jesus, and to become pregnant outside of marriage; and now, now You want me to go to hell for You!" Bowing graciously to the Golden

Throne, she continued, "But Your Will be done here in heaven as it is on earth. I accept Your invitation. But, my Lord God, won't I look out of place in hell, and won't they know that I . . . ah . . . ah, don't belong there?"

"Hmmmm," mused God. "You are right, my dear. That blue and white outfit of yours isn't going to work for this special assignment. You will need a disguise if you are even to get through the gates."

For a brief moment there was silence at the meeting, and then Mary Magdalen stepped forward and said, "I'll give Mary one of my scarlet-red dresses to wear."

Rahab, the prostitute of Jericho, who hid the spies of Joshua in her house and whom Matthew included in the family tree of Jesus, also came forward and said, "And I, my Lord Yahweh, will loan her some of my jewelry, earrings, and necklaces, and some oriental perfume from Sheba." As she was finishing her offer, Joan of Arc also offered to teach the Blessed Mother some four-letter words that she had learned while with the French Army.

Within moments Mary was transformed into a different looking woman. Joseph, her husband, leaned over and said to a saint standing next to him, "Gee, no one will ever guess who she is now!" To that, the saint replied, "No, Joseph, but they will guess *what* she is!" And so, with God's blessing, Mary of Nazareth, the Divine Secret Agent, left heaven for hell.

Since there is no time in heaven, it would be difficult to say how long Mary was gone on her special mission to hell. But about six rainbows later she returned, and Saint Peter announced her arrival. The word of Mary's return spread as quickly as peanut butter on a piece of warm toast. Within minutes, every saint and angel was gathered around the Throne of God, eager to hear the report of what in hell was going on.

Mary, still dressed in her secret disguise, began to make her report to the Lord God and to all the holy ones of heaven. "I must confess," she began, "that I was surprised by what I found when I arrived, and I am sure you all will be as well. Hell is one vast and enormous room. No one is alone in hell; no one is ever alone. Everyone is talking, but no one is listening. There is no boredom. The people there are doing several things simultaneously: like making love and making out their income tax statements at the same time; while others are eating their meals, watching television, and visiting . . . also all at the same time!

"Also in hell, I found complete freedom! Everyone is free of commitments and promises. Free to do whatever they feel like doing. Some days they are friendly and other days they are unpleasant; lovable one day and spiteful the next. And this lack of continuity or fidelity is not limited just to people. Clocks, flashlights, and hairdryers have the same freedom; some days they are faithful and work, and at other times they don't work at all!"

Mary paused for a second and, in that brief silence, a question came from the crowd that encircled God's throne: "What do people in hell do all day; what sort of work do they do?" People turned around to see who had asked that question. Jesus smiled when He saw that it was Saint Martha. Even up here in heaven, she was concerned about keeping busy. Martha continued, "They don't just sit around all day doing nothing, do they?"

"No, Martha," replied Mary, "that's another interesting fact I found in hell . . . they don't work. But while there is no work in hell, there is no leisure either. In fact, I found that life there is constant restlessness. They spend most of their time playing. Well, not really playing; rather,

I mean playing sports. A variety of games of competition is constantly in progress. Everyone is so occupied with winning, they fail to see that in any competition no one really wins. For if someone has to lose, suffering defeat and shame — as in the greatest game of all, War — how can anyone really win? And since there are no children in hell — surely one thing that You, Lord God, must have guessed — and since there are no persons for whom the child within them is still alive, there is no play in their playing.

"Finally, what impressed me about hell was that everything there was functional! Wherever I looked, I saw only that which was practical and functional; nothing was there just because it was beautiful. Beauty was absent, and one saw only efficient things. Everywhere I looked I saw plastic and polyester.

"Well, Lord God, that is my report, and I assure You that it was hell. No one, no one who is there is happy."

Again, silence filled the entire assembly as all looked towards God to see what would be done with this unusual report. After a long silence, God began to speak slowly: "My heart aches whenever any of my children are so unhappy. As Mary, my faithful servant, was giving her report to us, I made a decision! I shall remove hell from the universe and bring all who are there up here to heaven with me, where they can be happy."

This decision on the part of God was met with a long and loud applause, as well as a couple of toots from the trumpets in the angel band. But Mary spoke up and said, "Oh, God, Compassionate and Kind, even for You, I don't think that's possible! I failed to tell You the last thing I noticed while leaving hell. While there are gates on hell — large, ugly, iron ones — they are not locked or guarded . . . and for a good reason. The people in hell would not be happy anywhere else, even in heaven. They are where they are because they enjoy competition; enjoy seeing others lose. They enjoy being restless, having constant noise, and never being alone. They find pleasure in the absence of fidelity and commitment. They would find real beauty, such as a tree, unpainted wood, or the earth, cheap in comparison to polyester or plastic. No, my Lord, if You do not want them to be more miserable than they are now, You must leave everyone in hell in hell."

Not a single sound could be heard in all of heaven. Not a white robe or golden halo stirred as God, with a bowed head, sat in sorrow. Slowly a beatific smile spread over the Divine Face, and with that everyone smiled — for they knew that, once again, God had an idea! God leaned over and whispered into the ear of the Holy Spirit. After a brief exchange between them, God spoke with great enthusiasm: "Fellow citizens of heaven, one and all, if those in hell have, by their lives, shaped their hearts so that they are able only to live in hell, then I must send a redeemer to hell so that they can learn to live differently. Once this has been accomplished, then I can bring them to heaven and burn hell to the ground. I have decided to send a savior to hell! The person that I shall send must be strong, for it will be necessary for that messenger to live without any sign of my Divine Presence. This new redeemer must be able to live solely on faith, for if my presence were to be present, even in the tiniest way, even in the heart, then hell would cease to be hell. No, this minister of mine must be able to live without confirmation or consolation; to feel daily the sense of abandonment by me. To exist, such a redeemer must be a dreamer and be able to live on dreams and hope. Such a savior must be able to take today with its comforts, its security, and kiss it good-bye. It will take great courage, for the mission of redemption will require not one great, heroic deed — as it did for You, my Son Jesus, in Your painful Good Friday crucifixion — no, this new redeemer must be able to spread out suffering over years and years. Not three hours on a cross, but perhaps three times thirty years of sacrifice and suffering. Where shall I find such a messiah?"

This time, the question posed by God was not met with a multitude of volunteers or suggestions of possible redeemers. God broke the silence with a command. "Gabriel!" shouted God. "Bring me the Book of the Living. And prepare to once again carry my message to the children of earth. In previous times, in great crises, I have sent saviors to the world; as I did with Buddha, the compassionate one, or my delightful and lovable Krishna. I fulfilled my promise and in the later days sent to them, the suffering children of earth, my Son Jesus. But who do I send this time?"

As God's great finger ran down the pages of the names of all the living and those yet to be born, God suddenly stopped. The divine eyes sparkled in the splendor of ten thousand sunrises, and God said, "Considering the extraordinary degree of patience that this redemption will require — considering the long suffering, great faith, and the necessity for a heart large enough even to love those who are in hell — I have decided that this time I will not repeat the past, and shall not send my usual redeemer. No, this time, the Messiah I shall send will be a woman!"

The end . . . of hell.

The Prophet

nother Sunday morning Mass, the second one of his day, was in process as the old parish priest looked out over the congregation. The lector's voice droned on as he read a selection from the book of Deuteronomy. The words of the Lord Yahweh filled the cavern of Saint Casimir's Church: "I will raise up a prophet like you from among their kinsmen, and will put my words into his mouth; he shall tell them all that I command him. If any man will not listen . . . ." The voice of the lay lector, who on weekdays was the manager of the local A&P store, continued to drone on. Old Father Finny wondered whether anyone heard — and if they heard, did anyone care?

Each Sunday, waves of words flowed out over the people, and yet no one ever seemed to get wet! Like the farm market reports on the noon-day news — what did those prices for hogs, sheep, and fat cattle mean to non-farm people? Cattle-raisers heard and understood, but did anyone else? Or like the Dow-Jones report — how many understand, or even care, what those mystic figures mean: "up two points, off a quarter." Words, words, waves of words, and no one gets wet! If he, the pastor, were to stop anyone on the steps of the church and ask them what was said in the reading of this morning's Mass — could anyone tell him? And, he thought to himself as he slowly folded and unfolded the hem of his chasuble, could even I tell them what was read by the lector?

Suddenly he realized that it was very still and quiet. It was his turn; it was time for the reading of the gospel, and everyone in church was waiting. Father Finny rose quickly, walked to the pulpit, and opened the gospel book. The walls of Saint Casimir's Church listened once again, as they had listened for over fifty years, to the reading of the gospel for that Sunday morning. The faded faces of the saints, painted on the church walls, were as intent upon the "Good News" as were the faces of those who stood there restless, in neat rows, pew after pew. Father Finny finished the reading with the ritual expression "This is the Gospel of the Lord!" The congregation routinely replied "Praise to You, Lord Jesus Christ," as he kissed the page of the gospel book . . . when he felt a sudden sting on his lips. His lips were snagged! He raised his head from the gospel book. Whatever it was that had snagged his lips was now stuck to them! It seemed to be enlarging; increasing in size and forcing his lips apart.

Looking out at the congregation, Father Finny could see their shock and horror. Instead of being seated for the sermon, they simply stood there, gaping at him and at whatever was now stuck to his lips. The priest was unable to continue and was concerned about what had lodged between his upper and lower lips. He quickly left the sanctuary and returned to the sacristy. There he looked into the dressing mirror that stood next to the wash basin and saw a mysterious sight. Three unknown letters or hiero-glyphics were lodged between his lips. They pushed his mouth open as if three black, twisted toothpicks had been stuck there. The three letters formed a word that he had never seen before. Perhaps it was Hebrew, or even Russian — the word was UOY. What did it mean; why was it there?

Then the old priest realized that he was viewing the letters backwards in the mirror. The letters stuck in his mouth were not UOY, but *YOU*! While he knew what the letters were, he did not know what they were doing there or where they had come from . . . and why? Then he remembered the church full of people and that Mass was only halfway finish-ed. He quickly returned to the pulpit and, looking down at the page of the gospel, could see that three letters were indeed missing from the page. The three letters missing were those now forcing his mouth open. He stood in the pulpit and attempted to speak. His attempts were futile, for the trinity of letters prevented him from speaking. They had now grown to almost two inches in size, and only garbled sounds came from his mouth.

There was no pain, except if he attempted to close his mouth or tried to remove the three letters which seemed to be steadfastly soldered to his lips. Unable to preach, he returned to the altar to finish Mass. He was unable to say the prayers of the Mass and could only perform the unspoken rituals. That morning the parish did not hear another word from him, but only saw the word. That word, now trapped on his lips, was the loudest word ever heard in Saint Casimir's . . . "YOU." But no one, not even the priest, knew what it meant!

After Mass, everyone crowded around to help. Not even the A&P lector could manage to free the letters from his lips. Gesturing that all would be well, he sent them home as he returned to the rectory to struggle with the meaning of what had happened. Was it a curse? A diabolic possession? Some mystical experience? What . . . what was happening to him? He sat in his large, brown leather chair across from the staring, single, dead eye of the TV set and wondered: "Why, Lord? Why this word out of all the words in the gospel? Surely if a special word was to come, would it not be the sacred name of Jesus, or even the name of God? But this word; why did this small, unimportant word leap off the page and fasten itself to my lips?"

Sunday passed slowly. Time and time again he attempted to loosen the three letters, but without any success. He could not eat, but did manage to sip a little potato soup and drink some tea. As he fell asleep that night, he wondered to himself, "What will the Archbishop say about this?"

Monday morning came, but with it no solution to Father Finny's dilemma. He awoke with his problem on his lips and all of his questions remained. As the week passed, he tried prayer, force, and more prayer . . . all without any success. Friday morning it came: the call from the Archbishop. It seemed that a group of "concerned parishioners" had informed him of what had happened and demanded that something be done for poor Father Finny. His appointment at the chancery was for two o'clock that afternoon.

Naturally, he was a bit fearful and uneasy as he waited for the Archbishop — a kind and humble man who wore neither ring nor jeweled cross. Still, Father Finny was unsure of how such an unusual problem would be treated. "Who knows," thought the old priest, "perhaps an exorcism; surely this isn't the work of God!" As he waited for the Archbishop, he was thankful that he had never had to consider taking on such a task as being bishop. Who could ever match the requirements of such a job? It was wrong to speak of them being "elevated" to that position; rather, they were condemned to the role. Before the ceremony when they become bishop, there should be some sort of last meal; you know, like the ones they give condemned prisoners.

As was Father Finny's custom, he folded and unfolded the closest thing near him as he thought. This time he was folding a leaf of the philodendron on the coffee table in the lobby of the chancery. As he folded and refolded the leaf, he thought to himself, "Yes, Moses should be the patron saint of bishops. In their ritual of ordination to bishop there should be special prayers to Moses. He was both a mystic and a man of prayer, and also an excellent administrator. He could manage all those people, priests, and temporal affairs and, at the same time, he could ascend Mount Sinai and be alone in mystical prayer with his beloved God." Suddenly, in the midst of his reflection, Father Finny was aware that someone was standing next to him. He looked up, and smiling down at him was the Archbishop.

The Archbishop was gracious, but it was evident that he couldn't take his eyes off Father Finny's mouth. The two men entered the episcopal office and closed the door. The philodendron unfolded its leaf and gave a small sigh. Inside the paneled office, the Archbishop drew his chair close to Father Finny's and began to offer him a cigarette when, with a bit of embarrassment, he smiled and withdrew his hand. The Archbishop inhaled deeply from his cigarette and, again with a smile, said, "Well, Father, I understand that unusual things have happened at Saint Casimir's?" The priest smiled and attempted to speak, but only guttural sounds came forth.

The Archbishop held up his hand. "I understand; or

at least I see the difficulty. Perhaps it will be easier if I speak. We have a problem, Father Finny. I fear that, as long as your present problem remains, we cannot leave you as acting pastor of Saint Casimir's. The people are concerned about how you can handle baptisms, weddings, and even Mass. Personally, of course, I'm not that concerned. You are a holy man, and what difference does it make if you are unable to speak? We have too many words as it is in the liturgy; words piled on top of words. Who remembers all those words anyway? The most important things in life are beyond them. The unspoken and unspeakable awe, Father Finny — that's where the real Mystery lies. And so, you are unable to say a thing to your people . . . you can only be! Who knows, perhaps that's where the essence of the priesthood lies in the first place? Not in words, but in being. Who remembers the poetic, cleverly-phrased words of the eloquent speaker anyway? Who reads or listens to my words about social justice and care of the poor? Yes, Father, that's reality; but we are not in the business of reality, are we? I fear I must make some changes, so that a proper pastor can take your place at Saint Casimir's. I know you will understand. It's not only worship, but also all those important talks before the Lions Club or the Knights of Columbus!"

Still smiling, the Archbishop moved his chair closer to the silent priest and continued, "And you? I see the question in your eyes even if you are unable to form it on your lips . . . and what will happen to you? Father Finny, I believe that you are a prophet! Yes, I do believe that you have a message on your lips and a message that we all must hear. Yet, like all holy messages, we do not want to hear it! And prophets — those who have the mission of proclaiming the message — are, we might say, stuck with the job! Don't attempt to speak, Father. I can read the question in your eyes: 'What is the divine message contained in this simple and unimportant word that is frozen on my lips?' The message, I think, is a most important one for us who live today. We live in the 'me' generation. All around us is the continuous cry, 'What's in it for me? Please love me! Help me! Touch me, come to me . . . me, me, me . . . .' Everything is directed towards me and my needs, my growth, my happiness."

The Archbishop slowly smoked the last of his cigarette and then looked carefully at the old priest seated across from him. Father Finny was folding and unfolding a matchbook cover, his eyes filled with tears. "You, my friend," said the Archbishop, "you are a prophet of the most high; a madman, a fool with the holy coded word upon your lips. You can no longer preach the gospel, you must *be* the gospel! Come, please, and live with me. You can share a room in my home and perform whatever tasks you desire. But I want you near me. I want the people to see you. I want my priests to see you and to wonder."

It was not easy being an unproductive priest; not doing anything but just being. He even picked up a nickname: "Father You-who." That was a logical joke; the letters "YOU" on his lips . . . to whom did they refer? Who was the *YOU*? God? The person who looked upon the priest? Who indeed? And as is always the case, prophets are treated with humor, since that is the best of all defenses against the dynamics of their message.

Father Finny lived with the Archbishop for ten years. He performed humble tasks like caring for the yard, taking out the trash, and driving the Archbishop on the long Confirmation tours. He never spoke a word; he only announced like some human billboard the single word — "YOU."

With old age and heart fatigue, death came one day to the guest room of the Archbishop's home. As he lay dying, having received the last sacraments of the Church, and with his close friend the Archbishop standing beside his bed, Father Finny attempted to speak. He wanted to thank the Archbishop for his friendship and for all of his kindnesses over the ten years since that fateful Sunday morning at Saint Casimir's. As he attempted to speak, a strange thing happened: the letters began to reshape themselves. They formed into a single complex symbol. The Archbishop looked intently at the mysterious sign but did not recognize it, and then it completely disappeared . . . and Father Finny's lips were free.

Slowly, as if tasting rare wine, he closed his lips and then opened them. He was saying something, but so faintly that the Archbishop could not hear. He leaned closer, putting his ear close to the old priest's mouth, and then he heard so faintly, yet so clearly, a single word — "YOU!" It was the last word of the dying priest.

The Archbishop's eyes were filled with tears as he closed the eyes of the old priest and, slowly and prayerfully, drew the bed covers over his face. As he slowly walked down the stairs, the Archbishop couldn't help but remember something he had heard years and years ago . . . that, in the Orient, it is believed you will go straight to heaven if you die with the name of God upon your lips.

Jack and His Dream

Once upon a time, there lived a young boy named Jack who dreamed of being great. That's not a novel way to begin a fairy tale except that Jack dreamed of being a computer. The walls of his bedroom were covered with posters and photographs of computers. He read books about them and even went to see them in the offices of large corporations. Jack was fascinated by their magical, if not unlimited, power. "Someday," he dreamed, "I will be a giant computer. That would be better than being some baseball hero or some rock-music star!"

"Just think of it," whispered his imagination, "you'll never forget anything; you will be able to remember every telephone and license plate number, every name and fact you ever hear! And your powers of calculation . . . why, what would take a hundred scientists over fifty years to estimate, you will do in a split second! Best of all, you will never make a mistake as long as your printed circuitry is working properly. You will always have the correct answer. Power, fame, and wealth will be yours!"

Now, as so often happens in life when people dream and

fill their hearts with a single wish, that dream comes true. So, as he grew up and matured, Jack became a computer. No ordinary mortal, he became what he had always dreamed of being: an efficient, all-knowing computer. As a result, Jack was quickly promoted in his company. His qualifications were many: he never wasted time on coffee breaks, never slipped away for a siesta, and performed all his work with split-second speed. Jack never wasted time on such unnecessary words like "please" or "thank you," or even "excuse me, I'm sorry." Machines have no need for such terms.

The Board of Directors of the company had their eye on this amazing young man, for his gifts were so numerous. Not only was he efficient and hardworking, Jack was ideal for firing or correcting those employees who had errored in some way. The correction came from Jack in clear, right-to-the-point words. Since he was a computer, he was unable to shade his words with tenderness or humor. Ah, indeed, the truth does hurt if it comes from a computer. Reality without humor is strong medicine. The employees would shudder whenever they were told: "Jack wants to see you in his office."

Now you might ask: "If Jack worked hard, never took a vacation, and even if he never made a mistake, was he a happy man?" The answer, friends, is "well, yes and no." He wasn't happy and he wasn't sad. Jack simply was. Computers hum away to a special electric melody, and rejoice in frequent checkups and in being kept clean and well-oiled. Most of all, machines like Jack love to be valued. A special sensual thrill is theirs when they realize that others depend upon them; even to the degree that they would be helpless without their special skills.

Now, in all fairness to Jack, it is important for us to remember that he did not realize that he was a machine. The transformation from human to machine took years and years, and, of course, he did not look like a computer. Except for the computer keyboard that was located on his chest (hidden beneath his shirt), he was a most ordinary-looking business-man. But inside, it was different. In place of a heart was a small silicone chip that stored billions of bits of information, and in place of nerves were miles of electric circuits. Since Jack lived in a world of machines, he did not feel like an alien. A good number of his associates were also computers, especially those nearer the top of the company.

But everything was not as perfect as it seemed on the sur-face; there were problems. For example, when Jack would drive home after work he would on occasions see a sunset. The sunset could not be programmed. Oh, he could calcu-late the precise angle of the descent of the sun or even the heat ratio of its ultraviolet rays, but he could not taste the sunset. Jack found no pleasure in watching the sun gently descend into luminous pools of orange and yellow light.

And then there was the problem with music. Jack could list for you all the great composers in alphabetical order. He could give you the complete history of music from the cave to the concert hall, but Jack could not enjoy the sound of music.

He had once read that the "enchanted ones" could actually find sensual pleasure in watching the sun set; that these enchanted ones could be thrilled by the very sound of music, and have absolutely no desire to know the vast mathematical combinations of its tonal scale. Jack wondered what it would be like to be enchanted, and he found the thought to be absolutely frightening! He realized that every-thing for which he had labored so hard — his power, his very efficiency — would be in grave jeopardy if he would become enchanted. "No," he thought, "I must be very careful that I am never bewitched."

Being bewitched is the result of coming into direct contact with a witch. Now, it is important to remember that over the years witches have suffered badly from an unkind press. Witches are usually seen as evil, curse-spinning, ugly women. Wizards, since they have better press agents, are usually viewed as kind, wise, and magical persons. But male or female, enchantment is the occupation of witches and wizards. I have explained this wee bit of history because in the apartment next to Jack there lived a good and beautiful witch. Her name was Angela . . . actually, her full name was Angela the Enchanted. I might add that she drove a blue Toyota and did not ride to work on a broom.

Late each day, Angela the Enchanted would go out on her patio porch and sit in silence. After a brief period of time, sitting very still with her eyes closed, she would open them and drink in the sunset. The same pattern was followed in the morning. However, she would be on the other side of the apartment house sitting on a friend's patio. There she would taste the symphony of the sunrise. Angela also had powers of vision. She could see inside things. She could also hear silent music. Her powers were many — she was even able to hear poetry in the dripping of a kitchen faucet!

Angela was cheerful and happy, and friends loved to be in her company. It was great fun just being in the presence of someone whose profession was enchantment. Simple meals became feasts, mistakes were decorated with humor, and gentleness oozed out of her in all four directions.

Now it happened that our hero Jack, the computer, had to attend a formal dinner with the executives of the corporation. His boss urged him not to come alone but rather to bring a date, since the Big Bosses loved to see their employees as fun-loving, "normal" individuals. So, obediently, Jack looked around for someone to take to the dinner. He decided, even though he was a bit fearful, that he would ask his neighbor, Angela.

The formal dinner proceeded with perfect precision. Jack wasn't happy and he wasn't sad; he was pleased, however, that everything from soup to dessert was so orderly and efficient. At the table, Jack did not taste his food; he was too busy talking. Facts, figures, dates, and events all poured out of him with electric eloquence. Angela listened quietly, sensually enjoying her food, smiling, and looking just absolutely ravishing. The boss looked down the long table and beamed, "What a beautiful woman and — with that beautifully efficient mind of Jack's — what a combination that couple would make!"

After dinner, as they were driving back home to their apartment complex, Angela frightened Jack by asking, "Can we pull over and stop, and just watch the moon?"

Every fear programmed into Jack surfaced at once. "Angela must be one of the Enchanted Ones! God help me, what will I do if she tries to bewitch me?" thought Jack, as he slid over as far as he could to his side of the car seat. Jack immediately punched a key on his computer keyboard . . . the one marked "IBM EMERGENCY INFORMATION — CODE 107." Instantly the printout began: "Do not eat apples given you by strangers; do not prick your finger on a needle; do not remove the cork from a bottle found floating in the sea; do not . . . etc., etc." The list went on giving all the various forms of enchantment ritual. All this while, Angela was lost in the serene beauty of the moon as it rose slowly over the treetops, flooding the valley with pale, white light. While she did, inside her a song was being chanted. For you see, enchantment is the result of chanting. An enchanted person is simply one whose lifestyle is that of singing the same song. A spell was being cast and spun around Jack. Angela was not bewitching Jack, rather she was enchanting him. Jack had been bewitched for years. He had been IBM-bewitched. That was the paradox; it was Jack who was cursed and it was Angela who was enchanted. She had decided, long before this night (because she was so strongly attracted to him), that it was more important for Jack to be happy than to be important.

Angela's touch was powerful, and, for the first time since he had been a small boy, Jack looked at the moon and did not have a single fact enter his head. A shiver of fear raced up his spine, climbing three vertebrae at a time. It was so pleasurable watching the moon, but forbidden — if not also sinful — for a machine to find such sensual delight in an experience that could not be measured or programmed.

Angela moved closer to Jack and rested her head on his shoulder. As he watched the moon, she, with ease, unbuttoned his shirt. Her fingers slid inside to the computer keyboard on his chest, and she quickly typed a brief message.

At once Jack sat bolt upright, jerking with spurts of energy as red lights flashed across his computer screen. The printout read: "407 COMPUTER OVERLOAD; 407 . . . ." Jack couldn't understand what was happening. Angela, once again, gently typed the same message on the keyboard. This time, loud alarm bells began ringing, yellow and red lights zig-zagged across his screen: "606 CANNOT COMPUTE; 606 CANNOT COMPUTE — 407 COMPUTER OVERLOAD." Panic was written in Jack's eyes as Angela, for a third time, touched the computer keys and fed the same message to the mechanical maze inside Jack. This time, all the lights on the screen began flashing; bells and buzzers alternated alarm signals as information gushed forth in a confused unintelligible stream. Then there was an explosion. Clouds of white smoke with sputtering sparks flew out in all directions, and a loud, piercing screech from Jack shattered the peaceful night. He slumped over the steering wheel as if dead.

For minutes he was unconscious. Then slowly he raised his head and, turning, looked at Angela. She was smiling, and suddenly Jack began to smile back. Then, for the first time in years, he broke into laughter. The sound was the same as that of giant ice fields in the arctic cracking in the spring thaw. And then he began to truly laugh, and the laughter came cascading down in torrents, giggling and swirling around Angela and filling that moon-touched night. Angela and Jack held each other tightly and they never let go. In fact, they were married shortly after that date and they lived happily together ever after.

The End*

*"But," you say, "it can't be the end of the story! We never heard what it was that Angela typed into the computer that was once Jack!"

Yes, that's true, and if we really want to know, we might have to ask Angela. But we might guess, and in the process come very close to the correct answer. Try it: just ask yourself a simple question and you might know what it was that Angela fed to the computer that was once Jack. Take a few minutes to answer, take several if you wish, but just ask yourself: "What was the most beautiful thing that was ever said to me?"

The Beggar-Poet's Curse

Once upon a time and place, centuries ago in Ireland, there was a blind poet-beggar. He went from town to town singing his songs of verse and begging his scant livelihood ...
— excuse me, but here it is important that I interrupt our story to fill you, the reader, in on some necessary history. In Ireland, nothing was feared more than a curse; just as nothing was desired more than a blessing! Among the seemingly endless list of curses, the most powerful and feared were those of the saint, the priest, the widow, and the poet! The saint's and the priest's powers lay in the gift of their ability to bless, while the widow's and the poet's powers lay in the fact that they were powerless — the poorest among the poor and defenseless. Therefore, God would listen more quickly to their outcries. There were, I might add, all types of curses: hereditary, temporary, conditional, etc., and all of them tended to be most colorful, unlike the drab curses of the present day. For example, there was one that went: "May the Lamb of God stick its foot through the floor of heaven and kick your ass into hell!" Now that's a colorful curse! But we must re-

turn to our story about the blind poet-beggar —

. . . one Christmas eve, the blind poet was begging in a village nestled in a valley north of County Mayo, singing his verses and holding out his thin cloth cap for any gifts of kindness. It had been a bad week with few gifts of charity; his total earnings had filled only the bottom half of his beggar's cap. The streets, which earlier that evening had been filled with shoppers buying their last-minute gifts from the village shops, were now all but deserted. The poet stood outside the door of the town pub, hoping against hope for a kind gift or two. Then, suddenly, with a bang, the door of the pub flew open, and tumbling out came a crowd of drunken young men. In the mayhem they accidentally struck the poet and sent him flying end-over-end. The coins that were in his cap came raining down in holiday jingles upon the cobblestone street, and were quickly swallowed up by the deep cracks between the gray stones. As he crawled on hands and knees over the rough-surfaced thoroughfare, searching madly for his meager earnings, the drunken rowdies roared with laughter. Consumed in rage, he stood up, raised both his arms high to heaven, and pronounced a curse: "A Christmas curse upon this village be, upon this green valley and countryside . . . and may a hunk of the soul of any who dares a gift to give, be stone cold by even' tide!"

The poet's cry rang out so loudly — more clearly than the peals of the parish church bells — that his voice filled every cottage of the village. Knowing the great and awesome power of a poet's curse, the heart of every man, woman, and child was filled with fear. At once, everyone hid the gifts they had intended to give the very next morning. And, from that day forward, no one gave a gift for fear of losing such a hunk of their soul. The village gift shop went bankrupt and had to close its doors. Each year thereafter at Christmas, though the villagers all had Christmas trees, no gifts were placed beneath them.

But as the years went by, the people found it increasingly difficult not to give something, some token, at times such as weddings and birthdays. After much thought and typical Irish adjustment, they invented the "present." The "present" was far different from the "gift." In giving a present, the people didn't give part of themselves, they simply presented the other with some object: a ring, a pair of boots, a clock. But, of course, a present lacked the richness of a gift, and so they came up with the idea of paper wrapping and bows. To make up for what was lacking inside the present, they decorated the outside.

Now, part of the mystery of a good curse is its ability to hang — sort of invisibly suspended — over a cottage or village; sometimes for years and years, just waiting for someone to violate one of its conditions. More than mindful of this in their dread of the curse, the people of the valley never gave a gift. It had been centuries now since the poet's mishap, but his curse was still hanging over all their heads.

One Saturday morning, a wandering minstrel rode into the village on a brightly painted wagon with his traveling magic show. The minstrel knew nothing of the curse or the valley's long history of never giving a gift. His afternoon performance attracted a large crowd who delighted in hearing singing and laughter once again. He juggled oranges, sang verses, performed magical tricks, and entertained with puppets. When he finished his show, a beautiful young girl, who had been transformed in joy standing before his portable stage, clapped the longest and loudest. He had noticed her beauty, and now, deeply touched by her appreciation, he leaned over and kissed her on the cheek. Then he said, "Here, I give you a gift"; and taking a golden chain from around his neck, he kissed it long and tenderly and placed it around her neck. The poor girl turned as pale as death itself, and all in the crowd raced back to their cottages. Mothers hid their children, while fathers locked and barred their doors and closed the shutters of their windows in fear. The beautiful young girl attempted to return the golden chain and, weeping as she did, told the minstrel of the poet's ancient curse upon the village.

Holding her gently by the hand so that she could not run away, and speaking in such a clear voice that he could be understood by everyone hiding in the village as they peeked out from behind their shuttered windows, he said: "In every error there is truth; and in every curse there is a blessing. Your ancient poet did speak the truth. Indeed, each time you give a gift you do lose a part of your soul. But that's not a curse; it's part of the mystery of giving a gift. Aware of that mystery, each time you give a gift you should slowly kiss it on the top, whereupon a small magical door opens in the gift so that part of your soul can slip inside. Every gift contains a hollow, hidden compartment that allows the gift to be a carrier of the real gift — a part of your soul. And whenever you receive a gift, you must also observe the proper rituals. First, you must gently press the gift to your lips. As you do, you must inhale the real gift that rides within it — a part of the soul of the giver. Then you must rejoice in the gift itself. To know this is to know that in the giving of gifts there must always be a gift exchange, or else there will be created an imbalance in the soul of the gift-giver. Indeed, fair lady, part of my soul has been lost to you in my giving of the golden chain. If I kept giving and giving gifts without receiving any in return, I would soon be out of soul and as dead as a rose in winter. The exchange does not require a gift-object; for even gratitude, if it be real and loving, is a gift. Hugs and kisses, thank-you notes and prayers, are also made with hidden, hollow compartments. Remember that the soul of the giver is in every gift.

"God has gifted us with creation — every tree, rock, and bird contains a hunk of God's own soul. The most beautiful gift God creates is the human child. He molds each child out of clay and tenderly kisses His gift. A part of the soul of God thereby slips into every human person."

Looking deeply into her eyes, the young minstrel continued, "Indeed, fair lady, I am less a man for having given to you and, for the moment, am short of soul, but I'll take the risk."

At this, the young girl stood up on her tiptoes, kissed him warmly, and said, "Kind stranger and singer of songs, I gift you not only with gratitude, but also with a hunk of my soul!"

The two glowed with such beauty that the entire village was flooded with light. A great cry of relief and joy arose from every cottage as doors and shuttered windows flew open. Young and old began dancing in the streets, for the ancient curse of County Mayo was now no more. And that Christmas, beneath every tree, there were gifts galore. The young minstrel and the fair lady married, and they wandered together over hill and dale, forever in love and in song.

Children of the Way

Once upon a time, two young people, who loved one another very much, met one afternoon in an old and weathered wooden barn. Their voices slowly floated upwards into the blue-gray darkness while the barn's aged knotholes opened wide to take in their conversation.

"Do you want to go all the way?" asked the young man.

"Is it," replied the young woman, "is it really, all the way?"

"Yes, yes," was his reply. "I love you so much. I know there are those who would say it's wrong. But, for now, forget your dad and mom; forget the preacher. Let's go all the way."

The voice of the young woman filled the darkness with beauty, "That's not my worry, really; what I'm concerned about is whether we are capable of going all the way. It's not that I think we can't do it physically, I mean. But I can't help wonder if you can go all the way in love if you haven't gone all the way in other things. I ask myself, 'Have I ever been totally engaged and consumed by the beauty of a flower or by poetry? Has my heart, my whole heart, ever really heard a song or seen a sunset?' And you — whom I love so much — if I haven't gone all the way in everyway, can I then go 'all the way' with you?"

"O God," said the young man as he lifted himself up on one elbow and laughingly looked her in the eyes. "That's what I get for falling in love with a philosopher!"

"Don't laugh!" she said. "I'm not playing games with you or trying to mess up your mind; I really need to know. And I'm afraid we're not ready." As she said this, she gently kissed him on the tip of his nose.

"What the hell is goin' on here?" shouted her stepfather, as he flung open the large barn door. Sunlight fell like a ten-foot yellow wall upon the two young lovers laying in the straw. "You slut!" yelled the stepfather. "Get back to the house and start your chores. And you, you no-good trouble-maker," he cried, accusingly wagging his finger wildly at the young man, "get off this farm and never let me see you around here again!"

As they hurriedly attempted to dress in the midst of shame and shouts, her mother came running from the house. Her outraged voice chimed in with that of her husband: "Is this how you repay us for our kindness to you? Is this the conduct of a Christian girl? Well, young woman, you'll have to answer to God for the sin; you best hide your face in shame and start to repent! It's high time you learned how the Lord intends for us to live!"

For weeks and weeks the girl was not allowed outside the farm gate. Her days were filled with an endless procession of chores and work; and her mealtimes were the worst punishment of all. There at the table, her stepfather and mother fed her with shame and silence. Her stepsisters, however, were not so silent. They constantly needled her and teased her with nicknames like "Playgirl" or "Straw-slut," and they added to her household chores by being careless and creating messes on purpose. They would spend the afternoons in long, white dresses, reclining on the large, cool porch on the east side of the house drinking lemonade, while she was made to work from sunrise to darkness as "penance for her sin." She neither attended church nor went to the store; she didn't even go to school, nor did she wish to. Her stepfather had told and retold the ugly story about what had happened in the barn so many times on his shopping trips to the village that it became common knowledge to all. When people heard, they would only shake their heads and say, "What a shame. What are young people coming to today? I feel sorry for you, especially after all that you and the missus did to give her a good Christian home."

About four o'clock one afternoon the bell tower of the village church began to clang-out an alarm. The ringing of the church bells was joined by that of the telephones along party lines: alarm, alarm . . . this was the single message. The bad news raced from shop to shop and from family to family: "An invasion from outer space!" They or It . . . or something . . . was coming. What had been only science fiction for years was now a reality, for earth was being visited from outer space. Contingency plans for a counterattack were being made as suggestions filled the air on how to repel the alien assault. Some urged conciliatory moves, suggesting that white bed sheets be flown from every cottage and from the church as well. People from every house in the village and from out-lying farms began gathering in the town square. Mothers came clutching their babies, the menfolk came bearing rifles or pitchforks, and all came watching the empty skies for the imminent invasion. Everyone was gathered together in the square in front of the church. Even she was there, for in all the excitement she had forgotten her shame and joined the crowd, her eyes filled with wonder.

Piercing through the cloud of commotion that rose from the crowd came the voice of the preacher: "You there . . . yes, you! What are you doing here? Away from here, you sinful woman! If ever there was a time when we needed God to hear our prayers, it is now. Everyone, I say everyone, knows that God does not hear the prayers of sinners! Begone, sinner, and live out the shame of your lustful heart!" The crowd turned toward her, and she seemed to shrink in size with the scorn that came from their eyes. Saddened, she turned and slinked away. The voice of the preacher now rose to a pious plateau: "Come, brothers and sisters, we must pray for guidance and protection. Come, let us enter the protection of God's House."

With muffled murmurings, as when bathwater goes down a tub drain, the crowd funneled through the front door of the village church. Left behind, the girl dropped down on an old bench in the abandoned village square. The signs on the shops spoke to her with silent lips, while the blank stare of the store windows examined her. She felt absolutely alone. Her heart was filled to overflowing with pain. She felt consumed with isolation and an indigestible loss. Then she saw him . . . he was hiding in the shadows of Miller's hardware store, his head hung low. Not since that ill-fated afternoon in the barn had their eyes met. She ran to him, sobbing, "We're out here by ourselves, and the invasion is coming at any moment. Oh, how foolish we were that day. What are we to do?"

"Don't cry," he said, though tear tracks could be seen running down his cheeks from his sore, red eyes. "I've missed you," he said. "More than anything else in the world, I've missed you!" They held each other's hands and watched the late afternoon sky for signs of the invasion. A rushing river of organ music flooded from the church. "Onward Christian Soldiers," "Faith of Our Fathers," and other religious "marches" were blasted out to fortify the hearts of the flock in preparation to do battle with the aliens from outer space. As daylight fast began to fade, the young couple became filled with fear and ran to the church.

The vestibule was empty except for a broken folding chair that leaned against the wall, kept company by two wicker collection baskets whose long poles leaned against one another like guards asleep on duty. Through frosted glass on the oaken doors, which led from the vestibule into the main area of the church, all that could be seen were the backs of ushers who were blocking any late entry. The organ continued to pound forth in march tempo as the congregation prayed with zest.

To the right, steps led darkly upward to the steeple of the church. Hand in hand, they climbed rapidly, two steps at a time. At least here, up in the steeple, they also could be close to God in this time of great peril. Breathless, they reached the top of the tall tower. The giant bells now slowly and silently rocked after their long call to action. They, too, were breathless. Just then two pigeons landed on the ledge, having returned after being frightened away by the loud voices of the bells. The cooing of the pigeons seemed strangely peaceful and reassuring to the young people, as below, the organ was in duet with the preacher's bible-babbling. Twilight fell upon all the countryside as the first stars of night appeared.

The two young lovers sat with their backs against the belfry wall with their arms around each other. They were afraid, but they were together. In the presence of love, all fear is impotent. "I love you," he said. "I love you as strongly as the feeling of hate and rejection I felt from all the village, and more!"

"And I," she responded, "I truly love you."

"I know now what you meant that afternoon in the barn," he went on. "I mean, about going all the way. These past weeks I've been wholly consumed with pain, down to the tips of my fingers. It's strange, but even in my sorrow sunsets were never more beautiful. I would sit, for hours it seemed, as I absorbed the golden light into every pore of my body. I was totally penetrated by light: orange, yellow, and then indigo. I and God . . . were one. I knew that, as I had never known it before."

"I, too," she confided, "at night, in the darkness of my little room, prayed as I never prayed before. Not just some part of me, my mind or lips, but all of me prayed. Prayer poured out from every cell and tissue. My heart was filled with sorrow and, strangely, with God at the very same time. I couldn't feel anger towards the people in the village or even my stepsisters . . . somehow, I just felt pity for them. I was filled with forgiveness, and it was absolute, I'm sure of that."

From down below, almost smothered by the thunder of the organ, rose the words of a hymn. The words were empty from constant use and hollow from history, but there they were: "I am the Way, come follow me!"

"Now I understand," he said. "I am the Way, and the way is All the Way!"

"Yes, yes," she agreed. "I didn't understand either, but that was what I was feeling. Unless we could go all the way in everyway, we couldn't have gone 'all the way.' For it means loving, thinking, being to the very limits of possibility." And the pigeons began to coo as the two young people embraced and kissed one another.

Down below in the church, the sanctuary was cluttered

with promises of what people would do if God would spare them from the menace of outer space. Never before had the carved wooden angels, who held up the pulpit, witnessed such generosity or dedication from the congregation. The promises of gifts were blended with petitions for forgiveness. So involved were the pious church folks that no one noticed it at first. The steeple was throbbing and expanding. The timbers of the old church began to creak and the plaster started to crack. With a deafening roar, the church tower began to move. Resembling some giant Titan missile, it began to lift off its foundations, tearing away from the church, and to rise slowly into the night sky. The darkness of early evening was shattered by an explosion of brilliant light. The entire congregation turned as a single person facing the rear of the church, while clouds of dust and plaster rose like August thunderheads around them. The organ, which had been silent, began to play as if it were a hundred cathedral organs. The entire countryside was filled with the rising crescendo of Bach's Toccata and Fugue in D Minor. The organist clutched her throat in fear — for no fingers were at the keys. The organ was playing all by itself. And, together with the organ, the bells were ringing in full chorus as the church steeple, with the force of a NASA rocket, rose up into the stars of the night. The congregation stuffed their fingers into their ears at the thunderous sound of the lift-off.

As the white clouds of dust and plaster drifted away into the darkness, the congregation stood with gaping mouths as they looked upward through the giant hole in the church roof. The steeple continued to climb higher and higher, bells ringing, rising into the star-sprinkled evening sky. A thin trail of white dust drifted backwards towards the earth. Then they saw it. Just a speck at first, a mere pinhole of light coming from the center of the constellation Scorpio. Its size magnified by minutes . . . no, by seconds . . . as it grew huge, coming out of the southern skies, the shape of some great summer storm front. The light was brilliant beyond anything they had ever seen before. Slowly rotating, it seemed incased by millions of tiny portholes of light. The giant starship, or whatever it was, was now as big as half the sky. The feared invasion had begun. The End was here. The rising steeple moved in a direct path towards the great luminous object, and they could see that in the center of it there was a portal, an opening. To the sounds of the final chords of Bach's Toccata, the steeple entered the portal and disappeared. Then all was silent. The congregation fell to its knees and wept for its sins.

Inside the giant starship, the steeple had safely come to rest at the end of a long light-filled runway. The bells were silent as the young man and woman rose from their embrace. Luminous voices welcomed them: "Do not be afraid; come this way, you know the Way!" They walked through long corridors with white floors, walls, and ceilings until they came to two tall double-doors that opened to a room so filled with light that they were forced to shield their eyes with their hands. Through their fingers they could perceive a tall, beautiful human form who spoke to them: "Do not be afraid. I am the Way and I have returned just as I promised that I would. Welcome! You and all those who have found the Way shall live with me forever. Fear not, for you will become accustomed to the brilliance. Here everything is total . . . light, love, and also justice." With that, the figure moved to a portal that looked down upon earth. "For the others, as for you, it is now harvest time. Time to reap all the seeds that have been sown . . . ."

The word "sown" seemed to hang in silence for seconds as the figure slowly raised one hand and pointed it towards the village. The giant starship did not pause a pulse beat as a beam of light swept up the village and the countryside. All that was left was a dark hole, like a missing tooth, in the smile on the face of the earth.

The Mystic Mechanic

*I*t was high noon in Wakeeney, Kansas. The brilliant midday sun was barbequing the asphalt pavement driveway that led in and out of Joe's Super Service Station. Standing proudly in front of the small red and white filling station were the two gasoline pumps — Lead-Free and Regular — a duet of drinks for the parade of cars streaming up and down Interstate 70 that ribboned past Joe's Super Service Station. To the west was Denver. Hidden from view below the horizon were the snow-capped Rocky Mountains. To the east, past scores of small farm towns with their tall, white grain elevators, was Kansas City; and even further east, St. Louis. Right in the middle, so to speak, was Joe's filling station . . . with the cleanest restrooms on I-70!

To the citizens of Wakeeney, Joe was the best mechanic on the interstate. He was more than a mechanic and filling station operator — he was also a tourist guide, good samaritan, philosopher, and commentator on local, national, and even international events. Joe was a philosopher because he loved to ask questions of his customers; questions for which there were big answers or no answers!

Old cars and new cars, big cars and little cars, lumbering recreational vans and tiny sports cars — all passed through Joe's station. For each car he had a smile and a question. For some, a simple question: "Sure is hot, isn't it?" For others, more difficult questions: "What do you think of Einstein's theory for space and energy?" And for the special ones, he had metaphysical questions: "Is it possible to find peace and happiness in this life?" Yes, Joe had a lot of questions for which he was personally seeking answers, and he never tired of asking strangers at the gas pumps for their opinions. As each car would pull into his station, Joe would size up the make of the car, the year, and the condition, and then he would know from which category to select a question.

Well, as I said, it was high noon and all the pumps were quiet, for the station was empty of cars. Even I-70 was devoid of traffic when this car appeared from almost nowhere and glided up to the pump marked "regular." Now Joe, in his fifty years, had seen a lot of cars. In his twenty years of pumping gas he had perhaps seen 100,000 cars, but he had never seen a car just like this one. It wasn't new and it wasn't old. It wasn't blue and it wasn't gold, but it was a most beautiful car. Joe, together with the windshield wiper stand and the new tire racks, stared at the luminous car. From the driver's seat emerged a white-turbaned man who said to Joe, "Fill her up, please." Then the driver walked away from the car towards the restrooms on the south side of the station.

As Joe began to fill the gasoline tank, he noticed that the car wasn't empty; there was someone sitting alone in the middle of the back seat. With a smile as wide as the Kansas horizon, Joe leaned forward and looked through the open back window of the car. But no question was asked. Instead, only silence; a silence so still that you could hear sunflowers swaying in the wind on the other side of I-70. What had stopped Joe was what he saw in the back of the car. There, dressed in flowing white robes in the middle of the back seat, was a little old man. His ancient face was beautiful and his eyes sparkled with the brilliance of golf-ball-sized diamonds. As Joe looked through the open window, the little old man smiled. Joe felt as if he had swallowed a rainbow. "Wow," he thought, "what a marvelous opportunity!" At once his memory did an olympic jackknife and triple-spin dive into his conscious, subconscious, and unconscious, reaching deep down for the most important question he had ever asked himself. "Howdy, friend," said Joe, as he smiled at the little old man. "What is the secret to peace and happiness?" The beautiful old man smiled deeply at him and, once again, Joe felt as though he had swallowed a rainbow.

"Excuse me, how much do we owe you?" came a voice from some distant galaxy. Suddenly Joe remembered where he was as he stood facing the white-turbaned driver standing in front of him with his opened billfold. The two men quickly settled their business. As the driver slipped behind the wheel, Joe turned again to the little old man. With a serene smile, the old man spoke. As he did, the car began to slowly glide away from the scene. "The secret of life is that it is never . . . ."

That was all that Joe heard. He ran down the sticky asphalt driveway shouting, "Wait! Never what? Life is never what?" But before the sentence could be finished, the mysterious car, like silken smoke, sped away. Joe slowly walked back to the station, saying over and over to himself, "The secret of life is that it is never . . . ."

Days, weeks, months, and years went by as that incomplete sentence haunted Joe. Once in a while, if the right car pulled into his station, he would ask them, "How would you finish this sentence: 'The secret of life is that it is never . . .'?" Over the years he had collected quite a variety of answers like, " . . . is never dull," " . . . is never easy," or even ". . . is never on time." The years passed and, as Joe attended to the broken fan belts or thirsty, empty gas tanks, he could not get that unanswered question out of his head.

As people grow older they seldom change except to age a bit, but Joe began to change from the day that the little old man with the beautiful eyes stopped for gas. Unable to find an answer to his great question, he became more and more comfortable with all his other unanswered questions. Joe also began to take more time to service cars. He wasn't in any hurry to finish any task he was doing. Why, once upon a time he was so busy that he hardly had time to use the restroom, and it was one of the cleanest on Interstate 70! No more mad dashing from the garage to the pumps. Joe took his time. To Joe, the line of traffic on the interstate never ended, so why hurry? "Take 'em as they come" — that became his motto. He was never possessed by deadlines, although he often met them. He was a free man; free of the social obligation to finish what he had begun. The big sign on the side of the service station had been half-painted for over ten years now and needed to be completed. That new wall in the women's restroom, the one they had replaced three years ago, really needed to be plastered. One of these days he would have to get around to it.

Thirty years had passed since that hot day and the visit of the mysterious car. At eighty, Joe was a happy and healthy man. He found great pleasure in unanswered questions and in unpainted signs, not to mention countless projects at work and at home that had never been finished. Pleasure is like a good suntan . . . it shows. Pleasure with life was visible all over Joe.

Now, I realize this may sound strange to you. I mean that a man could find pleasure in life with so many things incomplete. Most people find satisfaction and pleasure in finishing tasks: "I've finished high school," "I've finished college," "We've paid off our mortgage," "This project is completed," and so on. Joe was different. Joe never finished things, rather he let things finish. He was, we might say, a master craftsman at that cosmic trick. As I said, Joe, at eighty, was still full of life, still pumping gas. He radiated bliss to all who did business with him.

One night, when the new moon had risen and was standing tiptoe on top of the white grain elevator of Wakeeney, business was booming at Joe's Super Service Station. Cars were lined up four-deep for service, and both bays in the garage were filled. Joe was halfway through telling a story when an unusual car pulled into the driveway. It wasn't new and it wasn't old. It wasn't blue and it wasn't gold. The wondrous, luminous car glided to a stop and honked. Joe looked up and smiled. He stopped pumping gas and said to his old friend, "Excuse me, Bill, I've got a little unfinished business to attend to . . . ." He slowly walked down the driveway, greeting his customers with a slight smile and nod of the head. As they looked on, he stopped at the back window of the car and spoke, then nodded and, with a great smile, opened the back door and got in. The car, like a silent blast of butterflies, took off into the night.

Confusion, bewilderment, and anger filled the Super Service Station. "Hey, I didn't get my gas!" yelled a driver. His old buddy, to whom Joe had been talking, called to the quickly disappearing car, "Hey, Joe! You didn't finish your story. You didn't finish what you were saying!"

Another of Joe's old friends, who had been sitting on a

pop case next to the door, slowly took his pipe out of his mouth and spoke: "Maybe that's it. Maybe that's the completion to that sentence that old Joe has been asking people for years — the secret of life is that it is never finished!"

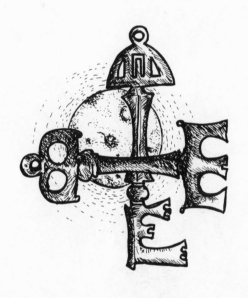

The Little Tin Box

*T*he long gravel driveway that led up from the highway was filled with cars and pickup trucks. The two-story, white farmhouse and large barn were surrounded by tractors and other farm machinery, together with furniture and a variety of household articles. The farm had been in their family now for two generations and, like so many other Midwestern farms, it had been sold recently to some European businessmen. Today, Tom and Mary would sell their furniture and all of their farm machinery. After trying different solutions, even a part-time job in town, Tom was giving up at attempting to make a living from farming.

The farm auction had attracted neighbors and strangers alike. The farmers gathered in small clusters, chatting about the price of cattle or recent futile efforts of the government to help farm prices. Their wives exchanged local news and gossip, but the general mood was sad. The auctioneer, a fat man wearing a white cowboy hat, stood on the haywagon and began the auction with gusto. The furniture went first. The antique oak dining room table and Victorian picture frames were purchased by strangers. After the furniture and antiques came the machinery. The large, orange Allis-Chalmers tractor, the combine, and cultivator changed hands to the Morse code of the auctioneer's chant. Most of the sale items had been sold when the auctioneer held up a small tin box and began his usual spiel: "How much do I hear for this small tin box?"

Before a single bid could be placed, Tom shouted, "Sorry, friends, the tin box is *not* for sale . . . everything else is, but not that!" He came forward and took the tin box from the auctioneer's hand saying, "Sorry, it must have gotten mixed up with the sale things by mistake." Tom walked away through the crowd smiling, with the battered tin box under his arm. The remaining items went quickly; the auction was over.

The day also began to quickly disappear as the long shadows of afternoon crisscrossed the old white farmhouse and the barnyard. The pickup trucks slowly rolled down the gravel driveway, the life possessions of Tom and Mary stacked on them or being towed behind. The ladies of the VFW auxiliary, who had served the sale with a lunch of sandwiches, donuts, and coffee, gave Mary some of the left-over food and drink. She carried them into the kitchen as Tom settled with the auctioneer, who echoed the sympathies of their neighbors about having to sell. He placed his fee into a worn-out, brown billfold and drove down the drive . . . the last car.

Mary was alone at the kitchen table as Tom entered the back door. The glare from the single bare lightbulb (the antique glass shade had brought a good price) made that once cozy room now seem as stark as a morgue. The house was empty except for the kitchen table and three chairs, and the large, old bed upstairs. The antique bed had belonged to

Tom's parents and was solid walnut. It and the table were not included in the sale, but had been given to one of their sons. Tomorrow he and his wife would pick them up.

Tom and Mary had planned on leaving the farm that night. Their suitcases and a pile of cardboard boxes stood ready by the door. The couple sat in silence at the kitchen table sharing the unsold ham sandwiches and coffee. The tin box had a place of honor in the center of the kitchen table. Mary was the first to speak: "They almost sold your little tin box."

"Yeah, that was close, wasn't it?" said Tom, as he slowly opened the lid of the box. To the average eye the box appeared to be empty, but in reality it was filled almost to the top. The old, battered tin box was filled with memories. Mary opened a suitcase and removed a small tin box that could have been a twin to Tom's. Slowly, one after another, they took out memories from their tin boxes and passed them to each other. One memory would awaken another one or be the leader of an entire parade of memories: "Remember the first night we stayed here after we were married . . . or when Dick came home from the Army . . . or that Christmas day in the '50s when we and the kids were snowbound?" Their little tin boxes held memories that went back to their early childhoods. In one corner of Tom's box was a memory of him and his friends, when they were young men, swimming in that deep pool down on the creek, the one that's surrounded by the giant cottonwoods.

These small tin boxes were what made Tom and Mary the richest people in the county. Early in life they had learned a great secret from Tom's grandfather. "The purpose of any possession," the old man had said, "is to make memories! The only purpose of money — only purpose — is to make memories. Things and possessions only rust and age, but

141

memories, Tommy, memories are like fine wine . . . they grow in value with time.'' Now that the farm sale and auction had completely dispossessed them of their belongings, they knew the wisdom of what grandfather had said to them in his funny, broken German-accent.

Tom returned the last memory to his tin box. He had to rearrange some memories for it to fit. He closed the lid and looked at his watch. They had visited over their memories so long that it seemed too late now and too much trouble to drive into town to their new apartment. Instead, they decided to spend just one more night at the farm. Mary unpacked some sheets from one of the cardboard boxes by the door and made the bed. By now the moon had risen and the wind blew waves of moonlight through the open windows. With no curtains or pictures, the bedroom was empty of things but full of pale, white moonlight. Tom placed his little tin box on the windowsill as he climbed into the ancient, great bed. Their last night on the farm was one of the most beautiful of their lives. Mary was asleep as Tom arose and stood by the open window. The fields, the barn, the windmill and, off in the distance, the cottonwoods along the creek were all silent but beautiful, bathed in the light of the giant moon.

Tom smiled as he opened, once again, his little tin box and gently placed inside it the memory of this beautiful night. He attempted to close the lid, but it wouldn't close; the box was so full. Gently he rearranged the memories so they would all fit. Then he closed the lid. As he did, it made a strange click that he had never heard before. Tom placed the old tin box on the windowsill and slowly laid back on the bed. He closed his eyes and was asleep almost at once. The next morning, when she awoke, Mary found him sleeping peacefully in the gentle arms of death.

The following days were hectic. The arrangements for the funeral, the arrival of their children and relatives, and the visits of friends and neighbors took Mary's time. Three nights later, accompanied by the family, she went to the funeral home. As they entered, the lobby was filled with many of the same farmers who, only a few days before, had stood in their yard on that auction day. They stood in small groups, discussing how selling the farm had been just too much for Tom. As she passed, Mary overheard their comments. She smiled to herself as she walked down the aisle towards the casket in the center of a sea of flowers, for she knew that selling the farm had nothing to do with Tom's death. Dressed all in black, she was regal in her serenity as she stood by the casket, looking down at her husband. Tom looked peaceful; his weatherworn face relaxed, his hands folded across his chest. His fingers still had tiny grease-darkened lines from all the years of hard work. Intertwined among his fingers was a black rosary. Mary opened her handbag and then, reaching down, she removed the rosary from Tom's hands and placed it in her bag. She then took from the handbag the little tin box and placed it in Tom's hands. The parish priest, who had been standing by the foot of the casket, stepped forward and, with his authoritarian but hushed voice (the one that came from years of speaking in the confessional), said to her, "Mary, Mary . . . you can't do that!" He started to reach down to remove the tin box from Tom's hands.

"Leave it there, Father Cryziski," Mary said, in an equally authoritarian and hushed voice, "that's Tom's rosary. Hardly a day would pass that he wouldn't take some memory out of that box and be filled with gratitude. He was a holy man, and he understood what poverty and prayer were all about. No, Father, the box remains because it's the only thing he's taking with him to heaven."

The priest began to object, but Mary outwitted him. She turned to the crowded funeral home, filled with people wall-to-wall, and said in a loud, clear voice, "Father Cryziski is now going to lead all of us in the rosary"; and with that she knelt beside the casket. The priest was trapped . . . and so, forced to kneel beside her, began: "In the name of the Father, and of the Son . . . ."

When the wake was over, and family and friends had all departed — even the Polish pastor who, while unhappy about the seeming sacrilege, had decided to let it go without further discussion — Mary returned to her apartment. Her black dress hung on the back of the bedroom door as she sat on the bed and smiled, thinking of how much Tom would have approved of what she had done that night. Then she carefully took out her own little tin box and opened it. She placed the memory of the wake — the many, many kind words about Tom, even the expression on Father Cryziski's face — all of it, into her little tin box. That memory fit perfectly on the very top of the full box. As she closed the lid, it made a strange little click. Mary smiled and laid back on the pillow. She was asleep, peacefully, almost at once.

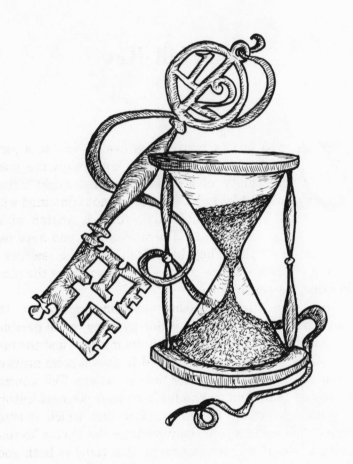

The Half-Key

While each story has been a key to a particular lock, is there not always the possibility of a Master Key that might unlock all locks? That story is not contained within this small book, for it is written within your heart. The stories that you have read are stories about life. They have dealt with the realities of life, even if perhaps those realities were seen from the inside rather than the outside.

Your own life, unfinished and incomplete at this moment, is the most perfect, if not puzzling, of all parables. Your own life's story is filled with the mystical and the marvelous. Only because you have lived it does it seem ordinary or even plain. Step back; take time to reflect. Tell yourself the story of you. And as you listen to your personal history, see behind the common and ordinary that which is extraordinary. See behind your daily routines the Divine Mystery weaving a tale of wonder and magic that touches both good and evil, darkness and light.

Since your life at this moment is still unfinished, it will be the most paradoxical and mysterious of all stories. But even though it is but half-a-key, it still holds the magic power to open the Gates of Paradise.

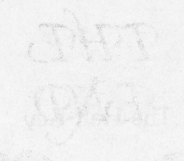

THE END

"What is the use
of a book,"
thought Alice,
"without pictures
or conversations?"

Alice in Wonderland

about the author

Edward Hays was born and spent his early years in Lincoln, Nebraska, but has lived in Kansas for the last thirty years. His college and graduate education was at the hands of the Benedictine monks of Conception Abbey in Conception, Missouri. Since 1958 he has been a Catholic priest of the Archdiocese of Kansas City in Kansas. For the past nine years, after travels in the Near East and India, he has been the director of a contemplative house of prayer, Shantivanam. Together with a fondness for peanut butter, movies, and storytelling, he enjoys and has tried his hand at the arts.